5.95

The NARROW GATE

Federico Suarez

SINAG-TALA
PUBLISHERS, INC.
Manila

©Original title in Spanish:
 La Puerta Angosta (Ediciones Rialp, S.A., Madrid),
 1971.
©English translation.
 Michael Adams, 1983
 This new Philippine edition was published in 1985 by
Sinag-tala Publishers, Inc. with special permission from
Ediciones Rialp, S.A. Madrid, Spain.
Nihil Obstat: Rt. Rev. Msgr. Victor R. Serrano, H.P.
(Censor).
Imprimatur: Rt. Rev. Msgr. Benjamin Mariño, P.A. (Vicar
General & Chancellor). Manila, August 18, 1977.

First Philippine printing (Revised English translation),
June 1985

ISBN 971-117-025-6

Contents

Introduction   7

**GOSPEL PASSAGES
ON WHICH THIS BOOK
IS BASED**

He who has ears to hear	9	*Matthew 13:9ff*
The narrow gate	17	*Luke 13:23-24*
With all your mind	25	*Matthew 22:34-37*
Do you also wish to go away?	33	*John 6:26-66*
The first stone	42	*John 8:2-9*
They did not believe in him	50	*John 12:37*
You will not have life in you	58	*John 6*
Being hated by the world	66	*John 15:18-20*
What is truth?	75	*John 18:37f*
The truth shall make you free	83	*John 8:31-32*
Crucify him!	91	*Luke 23:18-25*

Catholics and the Church   100

Hail Mary   109

Introduction

This book is simply a collection of talks given as meditations. Although it is primarily addressed to young people, to university students in particular, I think that it can be useful to all kinds of people.

I might begin by quoting some words of St Paul to the Galatians: 'But I wish I could be with you now, and change my tone, because I do not know what to make of you' (4.20). How should one speak to the youth of today about God and the Gospel? What is the language they understand? What are the right words, what is the correct approach, to show them the greatness of the task they have before them, the wonderful adventure involved in searching for God and discovering the meaning of life?

I do not really know. This is precisely why I have tried to retain the simple tone in which these meditations — if you can call them such — were born. I think that if they understood me then (at least some of them), perhaps they will also understand me now. I should point out, however, that being meditations addressed to Catholics, that is, baptized people who believe in Christ and who are members of the Church, the message they contain will not sink in unless the reader realizes that a Catholic has not only individual rights but also obligations.

Certainly — and anyone who reads these meditations will bear me out — it has not been my intention to play up to the youth of today (or of yesterday, for that matter). That kind of thing would be out of place and I think it would turn them off. I'm afraid I have gone to the opposite extreme. I firmly believe that since young people can give so much, much must be demanded of them. And I also believe, despite what may appear to the contrary, that if some people are struck by anything I have written, they will be men enough to accept it.

Today, when so much is being spoken about 'commitment' and 'standing up and being counted', I would like to see young people go against the tide and commit themselves fully to their faith, bearing witness to Jesus Christ no matter what. That is what this book hopes to do. I realize that this kind of commitment and of 'standing up and being counted' is no easy task these times. But they say that young people like challenges. God grant that this be true.

He who has ears to hear

At the end of the parable of the sower, there is a curious phrase which has always intrigued me. Our Lord, at the end of the parable, said: 'He who has ears to hear, let him hear' (Mt 13:9). He said this to everyone present; but later on he explained the meaning of the parable to his disciples. Notice: to his disciples, not to the rest. Why?

Surely the logical and reasonable thing to do if he really wanted to get his message across (and he undoubtedly did, since it was for this that he came) was to explain the parables as clearly as possible so that everyone, including slow, dim-witted, and even stupid people, would be able to know his doctrine. Nevertheless, only to his disciples did he make the meaning of his teachings clear, because 'To you', he said, 'it is given to know the mysteries of the kingdom of heaven' (Mt 13:11) but to the rest, to those who made up the great majority of his listeners, the only explanation he gives are those words: 'He who has ears to hear, let him hear.'

It is quite easy to make dogmatic statements about authors or ideas, especially when you are not an authority on the subject; this goes on all the time these days. Nevertheless, it is a dangerous thing to do, when what is in question is the Gospel: because the Word of God should not be turned into a mere object of ingenious intellectual dissertations, into material for brilliant and polemical but superficial essays. It should not be studied in the style of critics of literature, theatre or film who judge a work according to relative and personal criteria, which have much of the subjective in them. No one has the right to sit in judgement over the Word of God; nor should it be used as a vehicle for inculcating human doctrine of any type; nor does it need our cleverness for it to be of value.

No. The Gospel is something different. 'All that has been written', says St Paul, 'has been written for our salvation' (Rom. 15:4). He is referring to Scripture, of course. Scripture was written for our salvation, it is worth reflecting on it because it is the Word of God (and not the chatter of men) and, through it, God speaks to us so that we become better. That is why we will now try to understand this attitude of the Lord toward the disciples and toward the rest of his listeners, because there is surely some lesson to be learned here. Who knows?: maybe when we come to understand him, it will be much easier for us to understand ourselves!

If you pay attention when you read the Gospel, you will notice that usually a great many people gathered to listen to the Lord: 'crowds,' 'masses,' 'multitude' — these are the words the evangelists usually employ. Here, on this occasion St Matthew speaks of 'such great crowds gathered about him' that he found it necessary to get into a boat (they were on the seashore) and preach from there. Knox gives us a likely reason for his doing this when he could have spoken to them in greater comfort on land; but I don't want to go into that here; what I want us to do now is look more closely at the great gathering on the lakeside. What sort of people were there?

Three groups of listeners

We could, I suppose, classify them into three very distinct groups: the disciples, who doubtless formed a small group; also, probably, a certain number of scribes and Pharisees, a small representation of the religious establishment who carefully recorded, weighed and measured his every word; then, the people: men, women and children: ordinary people who went to listen to Jesus if he happened to be in the area and if they had nothing more important to do; and they listened to him with pleasure. Of course, these sociological divisions would include a variety of subgroups, but I still think that we can make these general distinctions because the presence of the disciples is certain, that of the scribes and Pharisees very probable, and that of the people quite obvious.

This means that there were a few people, the disciples, who trusted the Lord enough to follow him unconditionally, regardless of whether they understood him or not (often they barely understood him, as the Gospel explicitly states), but in any case they were ready to do what he told them. In other words, *they believed in him*. Other men, the scribes and Pharisees, neither believed in him nor loved him. They followed him, it seems, with a rather twisted intention. They did not like what he said nor the way he said it; they listened to him merely to contradict him or to find something with which to be able to accuse him. They did not accept that he had any authority ('By what authority do you do these things?': Mt 21:23), and, in principle, they were not inclined to accept any doctrine that differed from their own ideas.

The rest, that is to say, the majority, heard the Lord with pleasure; they were entertained, they liked his style; they were enthusiastic and, on occasions, they benefited by his miracles. However, they would go back to their work, to their homes, to their everyday lives. This multitude gave the impression of being made up of people who were casual listeners, who were not seriously interested in his teaching; nor were they inclined to make any real effort to adapt themselves to the message that was contained in the Lord's words.

Take it or leave it

So, only to a small group of listeners, that is, the disciples, was it granted to know the mysteries of the kingdom of God. But let us not prejudge. At the end of the parable, our Lord said to everyone (the disciples included): 'he who has ears to hear, let him hear.' It is as if he were saying, 'That's it: take it or leave it.' Why should he explain to them something they had perhaps no interest in knowing? He does not insist; he does not press them; he does not attempt to force any ideas upon them. He respects their freedom far beyond the way it is respected these days, these years when freedom is a constant topic of conversation and when we are endlessly bombarded with advertisements, slogans, catch-phrases and with high-sounding words from which no one can escape unless he goes to an isolated monastery away from it all.

When our Lord finished speaking, only a small group — the disciples — were interested enough in his words not to let them pass. To all appearances, the disciples were not particularly bright and many of the things that Jesus said escaped them. This is what happened on this occasion and so 'the disciples asked him the meaning of that parable' (Lk 8:9).

I get the impression that if our Lord left the phrase we read at the beginning hanging in the air, he did so precisely to allow his listeners to adopt whatever attitude they chose to: to take it or leave it, to be interested in it or not to give it much importance. Only the person who had real interest in knowing

11

what he meant would ask for clarification. Apparently only the disciples acted in this way.

They asked, but not in the way that the scribes and Pharisees did, that is, to argue with him or to find a way of incriminating him or of ridiculing him before the people, cornering him and putting him on the spot through skilful questions designed to catch him out. No. They asked with simplicity, without much depth, without any ill intention; they asked to learn, not to debate; to go deeper in his teachings, not to discover if it had any weak points. They never used their own personal judgment as the basis of truth, with which to resist the teaching expounded by the Lord. They simply asked; they listened to the answer and had enough material to reflect on for a long while.

This, then, was the way the disciples asked for the meaning of the parable, according to St Luke. But St Matthew does not say exactly the same thing; according to him, 'the disciples came up and said to him, "Why do you speak to them in parables?" ' (Mt 13:10). You can see that the question we ourselves asked at the very start of this meditation — no doubt a very disconcerting question — is not, after all, a new question, the fault of a twentieth century hyper-critical approach. The same question occurred to the disciples; but instead of turning the question into a problem, they simply asked for an explanation. And it seems to me that the reply they received is exceedingly timely for people of our times and especially for university people. He told them: 'This is why I speak to them in parables, because seeing they do not see, and hearing they do not hear' (Mt 13:13).

The difference between seeing and looking

What difference is there between seeing and looking, between hearing and listening? And what kind of difference is it that God should give it so much weight? A person absorbed in his thoughts may hear a conversation going on but be absolutely unaware of it: his attention is fixed on something else. He hears: the sounds reach his ears; but he is not listening. The same occurs with *seeing* and *looking*. We constantly see lots of things around us and yet they pass before our eyes unnoticed, as if they were not occurring. In other words, we do not look, we do not pay attention to them. In this case, also, our mind is elsewhere.

Attention, then, is what makes the difference between

hearing and listening, between seeing and looking. Those who see but do not look, and hear but do not listen, are those who do not pay attention to what is occurring before their eyes or ears. There are times when our attention is caught automatically by what we see or hear; our eyes and ears are attracted by pleasing images and sounds the way iron is attracted by a magnet. But this kind of looking or listening is more passive than active; our attention is caught because it is attracted and our will, our desire, expresses itself in a negative manner by not rejecting the thing. We might say that if there is attention it is because something pleases us, not because it really interests us. This sort of thing happens at lectures if the speaker is able to present his subject with enough skill to capture our attention.

But there is another kind of attention — the one born of deep desire, not the one stimulated by an external attraction. It is this type of attention we have when something really interests us, regardless of any instinctive attraction. For example, this is true of one who perseveres in learning foreign languages not because languages amuse him, but rather because he has a positive interest in knowing them. The genuineness of his attitude shows through: his attention is a true expression of a real interest and not merely a semblance of it.

The disciples had enough interest in our Lord's words (at least, that is how I see it) to ask and to learn what the words meant. The rest of his listeners, however, did not care one way or the other about the message his words contained. There is not the slightest effort or the least gesture on their part to suggest they had a desire to learn; not even the smallest sign that would indicate a mind open to the possibility that the doctrine that they were hearing could teach them something. The Pharisees' choice of a closed mind was simply the expression of their voluntary rejection of Jesus' message, because they did understand it on several occasions (the fact of disputing with him is proof of this). But not so the multitude: they did not reject the message of our Lord by a deliberate decision. Their lack of interest did not spring from a hostile attitude, from a voluntary resistance to being caught by the truth; rather it sprang from their superficiality. They were interested in other things. In their scale and values, there were many things that held their interest, way ahead of religious knowledge, even if this dealt precisely with the culmination of the entire history of the nation to which they belonged and with the reason for their being. Their attention preferred more immediate, more tangible objects. They weighed the importance of things by their immediacy rather than by their essential value.

This explains why only the disciples, but not the rest, were granted to know the mysteries of the kingdom of heaven. Among all his listeners, they were the only ones who asked the Lord, the only ones who showed interest to inquire what he really meant by that parable. They alone showed a desire to learn, because they alone paid enough attention to detect the existence of a doctrine hidden in the words they heard.

Superficiality

'Everything that has been written has been written for our salvation.' I rather think this is very applicable to us nowadays. If you look around you will find that the general attitude to the Gospel is not like that of the disciples: they were really interested in the Word of God; they wanted to go deep into it. No, I think that, in general, we would have to be numbered among that huge crowd of people, who have a rather passive attitude, who don't bother very much, if at all, to know the Gospel and assimilate it. Not that they reject it – of course not – or haven't got good will, but just because they are superficial. A superficiality, I feel, which in some cases stems from their conviction that they know as much as they need know, which is why it does not occur to them to think or read or inquire any further; in other people it is due, simply, to their not having time: all their attention is taken up by everyday affairs, to which they give great importance, because they are tangible and immediate, and they relegate to the last place (and therefore it never gets a look in) the only thing which really has decisive importance; in others, finally, this superficiality exists because the idea they have of what they were taught as children is so impoverished that they have no notion that it may contain something that is really worthwhile.

Superficiality due to vain self-sufficiency, superficiality due to sheer desire for comfort, superficiality due to prejudice. They do not find in the Gospel (or perhaps we ought to say 'We do not find'?) that attraction, that stimulus which captures their interest and attention. But our Lord *did* awaken interest, he *did* attract people's attention, and still only a few *wanted* to learn his teaching, only a few showed willingness to keep following him.

The importance of really wanting

I think that wanting, desiring, willing, is something very important. If you think about it, you will probably arrive at the conclusion that one person can do a lot for another. He can do almost everything, from thinking to sorting out his life for him. But there is one thing, only one thing, that no one can do for someone else: want. There everyone is absolutely alone, there no one can expect anything of others, because wanting, willing, is the act which is the most purely personal of all, it is the most genuine expression of the self, the self at its most unique. What is in question here is not being captivated or attracted by external stimuli to which one is not opposed (opposing is already an act of the will); no, it is a question of carrying out the most properly human of all acts, the free decision of the will as it follows imperative instructions from the intellect. A person knows what he has to do, and he does it. He is not drawn or led by any stimulus other than right reason and firm will.

Our Lord said and did all that he had to say and do; the Church has kept and taught his words with scrupulous fidelity and without alteration. It remains for us to do the second half of the job. Up to now, I fear, we appear to be more like that indifferent multitude, for whom what was important (as seen from their personal lives) was not our Lord or his words, but other things which were more tangible, more immediate, and — most important of all — more entertaining. This is what is most frightening about today's world, about many contemporary men and women; having the Word of God — their salvation — within reach, they exert not even the minimum effort to grasp it, to know it, to assimilate it, to live it.

Like that great multitude of people, we too are constantly seeing but it seems to me that we do not look. We hear continuously (has the Church ever spoken in terms as loud, as clear, as anguished, as she spoke through Pope Paul VI's words?) but we are not listening. Like the multitude during the time of our Lord, we too are preoccupied with some other business, with other things more tangible, more immediate, more entertaining. A concern for profound truths is not characteristic of contemporary man; in fact, the contrary seems to be the case: it appears that his psychological attitude is precisely to avoid having to take notice of God's message by spreading his attention over a thousand different things (usually of little worth). It seems as if modern man were trying to look away elsewhere, turning his head away in order not to find himself facing his

Lord. That this is due to ignorance, to superficiality, to prejudice or to selfish calculation does not change what is happening.

As for us who call ourselves Christians . . . perhaps you can assess how much interest we have in the Word of God, in the message of salvation, by assessing the interest you yourselves show, especially if you compare it with the interest you have in things that are much less important and which are not really earth-shattering. I believe we also give the impression, like the majority of those who listened to Jesus, of *not* being seriously interested, of *not wanting* to be interested. Or do we really want? The following words can perhaps serve as touchstone of your wanting: 'You tell me: "Yes, I want to!" Good. But do you "want to" as a miser wants his gold, as a mother wants her child, as a worldling wants honors, or as a poor sensualist wants his pleasure? No? Then you don't "want to".' (Escrivá, *The Way*, 316).

Well, I end here. Each one of you can reflect a bit over all that has been said: if anything succeeded in provoking some thought. But in any case, whether or not you reflect, the words of our Lord still hang in the air, like a call, an invitation, a reminder: '*He who has ears to hear, let him hear.*'

The Narrow Gate

I am sure you all know the expression used by theologians to designate the position of man on the earth: they speak of the *status viatoris:* he is in the position of a wayfarer. We are, they say, just passing through, on our way to a destination.

I don't think it calls for too much mental effort to recognise, at least in its general characteristics, that the 'provisional' character of man's situation on earth is almost a self-evident fact as far as each one of us is concerned. There was a time when we did not exist and history kept rolling on in spite of our not being here. Nobody missed us, nobody could miss us. After a while (a little while or a long while; it doesn't matter: it will always be a short time, hardly a puff) we'll die and you can rest assured that absolutely nothing will happen. Mankind will carry on more or less as before and except for a few people, and for a short while, nobody will miss us.

So, from one point of view and looking at things as a whole, this is what we are as we pass through the world: we are like a piece of time which begins, lasts a little and ends; it begins when we are born, it lasts over our life-time and it ends in death.

The first consequence of all this, if we think about it, is that this temporal character of man is a fact, not a theory; it is a fact which does not depend on us, we can do nothing about it. This brings us to one conclusion: we are not independent beings. The fact of our being born, and being born in a particular period of time, having specific parents, and certain endowments: this is not something we have willed. Nor does our dying depend on our will: we will inevitably die whether we like it or not, whether we want to or not. Independently of us and before we came into being, there was a reality into which we were inserted when we were born; this is something we can recognise, accept, reject, ignore or fight against, but we can't get rid of it: it is just there, independently of our will and there is nothing we can do about it. Man, whether he likes it or not, is a creature, a created being endowed with intelligence and freedom — and a being with a destiny which he ought to achieve by using that intelligence and freedom.

This destiny is his goal and it is to be found at the end of the road. Not on the road, but at the end, when the road runs out. That's why it is a goal. It is a destination, therefore, which is not in time but outside time, at the end of each person's time: not in this life, which is a way, but beyond it, at the end of life on earth. In other words, completeness, to which every rational being tends as a consequence of the way God has arranged things, can only be achieved after death when all human limitations have been left behind.

However, although man's destination is a marvellous goal, so marvellous that 'eye has not seen, nor ear heard, nor has it entered the heart of man to conceive what God has prepared for those who love him', this doesn't mean that he will *necessarily* reach his goal. He will reach it *if he wants to,* and he will not reach it if he doesn't want to. St Augustine put it very clearly and concisely when he wrote, 'God, who created you without you, will not save you without you.'

An inescapable choice: self or God

Life, then, the time we exist on earth, is the opportunity given every man called into existence to use his intelligence and his freedom (that's what makes him man) to work out his own eternity; to accept the destiny marked out for him, or to refuse it and choose one of his own making. Life is so arranged that you have to define yourself. The choice is inescapable. There are two things a man has necessarily to choose between: God and himself. Saying 'yes' to God means saying 'no' to oneself; and asserting oneself means denying God. One is free to choose; God, who never turns his back on what he has made, respects man's freedom and leaves him with whatever he freely opts for.

At the end of our way through time is death: it is the door that opens onto eternity, and then there is no more time. Every person will then be left with whatever he has chosen; if he has chosen God, then he will have God for all eternity and he will have reached the goal he sought and for which he worked; he will have God and he will also have found himself in the fullest possible sense. But if a person opts for himself and persists in this option despite all the callings he receives from God, despite all the opportunities which, one after another, are offered him to help him correct his mistaken choice, then he too will get what he was looking for: frustration, an eternity without God, where he is alone with himself — which is the same as saying that he won't even have found himself, for he will be lost.

So, there are two ways — and only two — a person can follow during his life on earth; all paths end up on one or other of these two roads. There is a narrow road, the road of saying 'no' to oneself; and a wide road, where one says 'yes' to oneself; a narrow gate, which is Jesus Christ ('I am the gate. He who enters by me will be saved') and a broad gate, 'the prince of this world', incompatible with Christ, opposed to Christ. A narrow road and a wide road: 'and many are those who follow it': naturally, it is much easier.

I think that some of this can be deduced from the Gospel, which twice refers to the narrow gate. On one occasion Jesus used this expression to reply to an indiscreet (not to say impertinent) question: 'Master, is it true that only a few will be saved?' He replied to them, 'Try your best to enter by the narrow gate, because, I tell you, many will try to enter and will not succeed' (Lk 13:23-24). And Matthew mentions it as part of the sermon on the Mount (Mt 7:13-14).

I find this bit very interesting: 'Many will try to enter and will not succeed'. I don't doubt but that in principle everyone, without exception, if allowed to choose between completion and frustration, heaven or hell, salvation or condemnation, love or hatred, would choose completion, heaven, salvation and love. It is not even conceivable, rationally speaking, for someone deliberately to choose frustration, condemnation, hell and hatred (and for all eternity!); pure, naked evil can never be the object of man's will, of man's love.

The only thing is that this does not get us very far — I mean this wanting something in a theoretical way, in principle. If we look at things not as pure theory but with reference to real life, it may be easier to understand. If a university student wants to be a doctor, he doesn't register for Roman philology: to learn medicine he doesn't need to study early Latin grammar or literary criticism; he has to do other subjects, which aren't taught in the Arts faculty. The fact is that if a student registers for Roman philology he is showing that what he really wants to be is a philologist, not a doctor, no matter what he may say, because his real objective, his love, is shown not by what he says, but by what he does.

And this is due to the fact that if you want something you

have to use suitable means to obtain it. Not any old means, but precisely those means which lead to the goal you are seeking, the objective you are aiming at. From this it follows that if you examine the means a man uses you can find out what goal he is pursuing. If someone says that he wants to go home and he deliberately chooses the road which leads to his enemy's house, then undoubtedly what he really wants is to go where, according to what he *says,* he doesn't want to go. And if the reason given is that the latter road is much easier, then what he really wants is that road: he is not in any way worried about where it leads.

The wide road, the narrow road. Well, it's not very difficult to see that in fact there are many who go along the wide road, in spite of its leading to perdition (as the Gospel says). Anyway, it's quite clear, especially in today's world, which so forcefully affirms man, his dignity and his rights (even Vatican II does this), that the expression 'denying oneself' — the first condition which the Lord demanded of his disciples — does not make much sense to the public at large. Nowadays what people are looking for is the affirmation of man. 'Finding oneself, discovering onself' is an aim of quite a lot of young people today: of those who never do manage to work out where they are; of those whose attitude gives rise to conflict between the older and younger generations and to very odd, rootless forms of existence.

It might be useful at this point to clarify a few concepts. In general, what one has not learned one does not know, and there are expressions whose meaning is easily grasped by people who are familiar with the truths to which they refer but which are unintelligible, confused or a source of scandal to those who have very little contact with them.

Every person has a false ego

Man messed up (if I may speak like that) God's plan by sinning. God created him in his own image and likeness and, in God's plan, the trajectory his life on earth should have taken is very different from what it now is. So the birth in sin of every man is the birth of a man with a false ego, as Merton put it. Not with the ego which God had meticulously planned for him but with the one which sin has impressed upon him. He is born, then, like someone who never was destined to be at all: he is as it were a falsification of himself, he is the deformed image of what in God's mind he ought to be and indeed is. He is, we could say in theological language, the 'old man' St Paul speaks of, that false being which should make way for the 'new man' who is the genuine image of God, once he has been despoiled of all falseness.

When young people of today — university students, workers or drop-outs — try to find themselves, I think they are trying to do something very important, although maybe they do it in darkness and without knowing how or where to go to find the answer. Finding one's true ego, one's true identity, is, indeed, a serious task and an objective well worth striving for. Merton writes (this is a translation into Spanish and then back into English): 'Those who know nothing about God and whose life is centred on themselves, think that they can find themselves only by asserting their desires, ambitions and appetites, in a struggle against everyone else. They try to become real persons by imposing themselves on others, by taking over part of the limited supply of created goods, and in this way underlining the difference between themselves and other people who have less than they do, or nothing at all.'

This self-assertion is the equivalent of the affirmation of the false ego, the affirmation of the old man. Merton describes one way, perhaps the most obvious one in today's consumer society, of asserting oneself, but there are others. In every case, however, what they have in common consists precisely in emphasising personality by throwing up barricades, by creating distinctions which differentiate one from others. The aim is to be different, to stand out: success, power, wealth, or new experiences, new ways of living which, by being so different, are a kind of challenge — even to the extent of using drugs and peculiar forms of dress so you can shout that you are not like other people, you are not conventional, you are authentic, there is no reason for you to subject yourself to pre-established forms created by others.

This is all doomed to failure. None of these things are able to make a man richer — but they can gradually, and without his realising it, make him poorer and more empty. It's only logical, for by enslaving oneself to things which are dead and in themselves meaningless, a man is impoverished and left empty and with nothing worthwhile to live for. There is a kind of person, buoyant and triumphant, who gives the impression that he is trying at all costs to anaesthetise his soul either by pouring himself into everything that's happening or by going for whichever form of escape is most accessible to him (alcohol, sex, drugs or theories). As far as those young people are concerned who try to find themselves by looking for new experiences or to assert themselves by rebelling and protesting in minor causes (which they think are great issues), this sometimes leads to great sadness, especially when at the age of twenty or twenty one (or even earlier) they have tasted everything and have lost all their yearnings and idealism and have become prematurely old, living a barren life which is good for nothing because it does no one any good.

The road to full development

However, paradoxical as it may seem, it is not the wide road of self-assertion which allows a person to find himself and fully develop his own personality. It is the narrow road that does that, the road of denying yourself, which means affirming God, because only by this narrow road and through the narrow gate — through Christ Jesus — can one achieve the death of the old man, the false ego, and the birth of the new man, the genuine personality. What I want to say to you can be summed up in a few words from *The Way:* 'We are blocks of stone that can move and feel, that have a perfectly free will. God himself is the stone-cutter who works on us, chipping off the rough edges, shaping us as he desires, with blows of the hammer and chisel. Don't let us try to draw aside, don't let us want to escape his will, for in any case we won't be able to avoid the blows. We will suffer all the more, and uselessly: and instead of polished stone, ready for the work of building, we will be a shapeless heap of gravel that people will trample contemptuously under foot' (J. Escrivá, *The Way*, 756).

And the reason for this is that life is made up of a continuous and constant succession of choices: the narrow path or the wide road, affirmation of God or assertion of self, the hardness of struggle or *la dolce vita,* the slippery slope towards the easy way. And at every moment, in every situation, in each of one's actions, one has to opt for one way or the other, for what is easy or what is difficult.

Well, then: on this choice you make at every hand's turn depends the general direction your life is imperceptibly acquiring; and it also determines the general shape your personality is acquiring; or, to put it the way Merton does, every event in one's life, every one of the moments which go to make up one's existence, plants a seed in man's soul. Some people — I think that they are unfortunately very few, although they could be very many — are able to catch this seed and tend it, until it develops and gives fruit; but in most people, to my mind, these seeds remain unfruitful. They die due to neglect or maybe they are just rejected, repelled by a hard heart or wasted by someone who is not interested in this kind of treasure. And so, interiorly, every man is making himself or unmaking himself; he is gradually becoming richer or poorer: everything depends on his interior attitude, on his reaction to things and events. When he chooses the narrow way, every time he denies himself, this helps strengthen his true personality, his genuine ego; every step he takes along the wide road lays a new layer of artificiality onto his own ego, because it means moving away, once more, from the genuine image of God each of us is, *whether we like it or not.*

The fact is that things and events, this whole ensemble of beings and facts we are constantly rubbing shoulders with, require of us a response. They are like blows of that hammer and chisel, sometimes hard and painful, at other times gentle and soft; and on our attitude, on our reaction, depends whether on each occasion, we shed a bit of our false ego or, on the contrary, strengthen a little the falseness we were born with. A suitable choice at the right moment can really put a man's life on the right track; a mistaken (however comfortable) choice can, on the contrary, turn the rest of his road into a slippery slope, where he can hardly keep his feet. And when a man reaches the end of the road and looks back at the route he's travelled, what he wants to see is not a heap of useless ruins.

A new world is in the making

I think that today it is very important — perhaps more so now than in more peaceful periods of history — for us to know what exactly is happening. We are experiencing the gradual destruction of the 'modern' world, a world born at the Renaissance and which has at last petered out, and at the same time we are experiencing all the pains which accompany every new birth.

Today it seems as if the young people who are shouting and moving around have great ideals and are chasing after high and ambitious goals. They want to change the structures, to build a new world (of course, one which is better than the present one) which is more just, less hypocritical, more disinterested. Not a brave new world like that described by Aldous Huxley but one which is more human, a world with a heart. This is — or so it seems — the great goal of young people.

But what about the road? What road do they have to take to get there? Notice: there is a job of building to be done. And building calls for effort, and tenacity; it calls for intelligence. This is a narrow road. You can never build anything by tearing down and destroying; but you must admit that destruction is much easier, quicker and more comfortable and calls for less (or no) intelligence. It is a wide road at the end of which all you find is a pile of rubble, ruins which cannot give us shelter.

On you rests the responsibility (or part of it, anyway) to *make* this world, which is being born, more just, more human, and to put more heart into it. You are the instruments which ought to build these new conditions in which your children will have to grow up (I trust that you are not among those who are more interested in ideologies than in people). But only those of you who are able to choose conscientiously and deliberately the narrow way — the way of difficult duty in place of easy escape — knowing what it entails, will be builders.

A road to be followed, an opportunity to seek completion or frustration, to build or to destroy; a life which cannot but be lived, and a choice that must be made. But do not forget that in this unique opportunity which life is, you gamble everything, here and hereafter, by the choice of road and goal.

With all your mind

In St Matthew's Gospel (22:34-37) we read the following: 'But when the Pharisees heard that he had silenced the Sadducees, they came together. And one of them, a lawyer, asked him a question, to test him. "Teacher, which is the greatest commandment in the law?" And Jesus said to him, "You shall love the Lord your God with all your heart, and with all your soul, and with all your mind." '

It is easy to notice here, as on other occasions, that the man who put the question was insincere. He wasn't looking for knowledge: he wanted to test Jesus, to put him in a compromising situation. But the answer he got was absolutely sincere; it was given clearly and directly, ignoring the hidden intention of the questioner. The answer is well-known to all of you but it contains a phrase which I think is of special relevance to Catholics today, and particularly to students, to those who work with their mind.

'You shall love the Lord your God with all your heart, and with all your soul, and with all your mind.' *With all your mind.* What does it mean to love God with all your mind? I don't know if you have ever asked yourself this, but anyway it's probably worth thinking about a little: certainly I think it needs going into.

Can you love what you do not know?

Let's begin by asking ourselves: Can you love what you do not know? Can you desire something you do not know? The philosophers reply: No, you can only desire something if you know it in some way or other. Knowing and wanting, having and loving, are so linked together that the act of the will — wanting — is somehow dependent on your mind. From this it is easy to see that the greater your knowledge the deeper your love. Or, in other words, the attitude of your will towards anything is dependent on the knowledge you have of that thing. If the mind makes a mistake and presents as good something which in fact is not good it puts the will in the position of having to make a wrong choice of going for something bad, which it takes in its stride because it is presented to it as good. And the other way round: if the mind mistakenly regards something good as bad and shows it to the will in this light, the will can reject it because of the quality of non-good projected onto it. So it is important for our knowledge to be true; on this depends the correctness of every choice we make, and therefore the full use of our freedom.

The mind, then, is a kind of governor in man's complex make-up. A man's conduct, the attitude he adopts towards God, the world, and other people, depends to a great extent on the ideas he has. And these ideas he usually learns, rather invents — especially his ideas about revelation, about God's message of salvation to men.

You will, I am sure, have noticed that God did not reveal himself to men all in one go. Being God, how could he? When the chosen people left Egypt they were little more than a horde — not even a people — incapable of understanding the most elementary and simple truths about the supernatural world; to give them the fulness of revelation would have meant burdening them with something they could not carry. With infinite patience and over hundreds of years, first through Moses and then through the other prophets whom he raised up, God set about preparing their minds. In this way, in the fulness of time, the people he had chosen would be capable of recognising his envoy and grasping the message of redemption. In fact it is even possible, in Jesus' own words in the Gospel, to distinguish the gradual unfolding of God's teaching. When he begins to preach, our Lord refers to the old law ('You have heard it said . . .') and he recalls the precept: 'You will love your friend and hate you enemy'; now, centuries later, the chosen people were ready to take a step forward, and Jesus, who had come to fulfil and complete the law (' . . . but I say to you') opens up new horizons and perfects the law: 'Love your enemies, do good to those who hate you, pray for those who abuse you . . .'

We are made in such a way that we can reach the truth only in a gradual way; this holds good for man in himself (his learning has to keep pace with his physical and mental development: a persons's intelligence is not the same at six as at thirty) and for the content of his knowledge (we cannot grasp complex things if we have not first got a grasp of elementary ideas).

A developing knowledge of God

Now let us look at the first question. What should we understand by 'You will love God with all your mind'? What is the Gospel saying?

I don't say that I can give a certain, complete answer. That, I think, would mean taking over the Church's role: only the Church can explain the exact meaning of Jesus' words without any risk of error. Yet, it is true that these words contain a teaching meant for all of us, a teaching which is not just confined to the intellectual sphere but which affects especially our life. So, reflection on these words, or any other parts of the Gospel, is the normal way of going deeper into the message of salvation.

But this deepening, or, if you wish, this knowledge, has to suit each person's intellectual development. You cannot give to an eleven-year-old the same textbook on geometry as is used by a third or fourth year maths student at university. Clearly intelligence undergoes a considerable development between the years of eleven and twenty and the university text seems as big to the child as the school text is small to the university student.

Very well then: when a child goes to make his first communion, he has learned the catechism but not the small print. He has a knowledge of God and of the supernatural world which is perfectly suited to his mental development; he knows as much as he can know at that age about the basic truths. And, what is more, his knowledge is on a par with his secular knowledge. There is no disproportion between what he knows about God and what he knows about men and things — nor is there any difference in the way he knows all these. I would say that the child loves God 'with all his mind.' because his knowledge of God is as complete as it can be. It reaches the limit of his intellectual ability at that stage in his development.

As a person's intelligence develops he grows in knowledge of the world and of life. A suitable programme of studies keeps opening up his intellectual horizons, and normal biological and psychical growth, social relationships and things that happen to him, all play a part in shaping his mind through the ideas he acquires in books, cinema, and television, conversations and experience. Usually, as far as his studies are concerned, he follows a plan which takes into account his mental development, the knowledge he has already acquired and the relative importance of the different subjects; everything is pretty well planned. His intelligence grows, so does his experience and his knowledge of the world and of things. Does his knowledge of God and of the supernatural world grow to the same extent?

From what I can see at the university and elsewhere the answer is: No. The average university student's knowledge of his faith is clearly on a lower level than his intellectual capacity and secular knowledge, and this is even true of people who are at the top of their class. You can quite often meet a scholar who knows everything, or almost everything, about his subject and nothing, or almost nothing, about the faith he professes. A German sociologist, Dieter Oberndörfer, has pointed this out — but it is something you can see for yourselves quite easily, whenever the conversation turns around these subjects.

The way we grasp the truths of faith

Generally speaking, a university student (at least in the country I live in) tends to think, especially if he has been to a Catholic school, that he 'knows it all' as far as the faith is concerned: he thinks that because he has learned the articles of faith in a particular, well-defined way there is nothing more to it. And in a way he is right, for there are few dogmas, and you can't find more over the horizon: revelation was closed with the death of the last apostle. He makes his mistake in confusing the *number* of truths of faith which he holds and the *way* in which he as a particular individual holds them. And also he is missing out on the connection between these truths and his real life — for revelation is no mere speculative system. It is an expression of realities which affect the core of one's personality, the world which surrounds him and in which he lives, and his ultimate and definitive destiny.

As far as the first point is concerned, that is, the *way* in which he has a hold of the truths of the faith, we should remember what we have already noted: only when one's knowledge of God and of revelation is on the same level as one's mental development and grasp of human knowledge is one fulfilling the commandment (if it can be called that) of loving God with all one's mind. But in the case of the average university student this is definitely not the case, for his religious knowledge tends to stop when he is thirteen or fourteen (rarely after that age does he continue to read books which are attuned to his development). He doesn't work at it after that age. The result is obvious: when he is twenty or twenty five (or older) he is still discussing subjects connected with the faith using concepts which suit a twelve-year old. He has learned nothing since then; in fact he has forgotten part of what he knew. And so it happens (even more often in these times of crisis) that when he tries to solve some problem of faith with his childish knowl edge, he finds the argument, the apologia, ridiculous (for it is childish) and the problem logical (for it is the result of a much more developed outlook and general education). In fact it is my own view that a very high proportion of the crises of faith which you meet among university students (I refer to honest crises, not the other kind) are rooted in the solid, increasing ignorance of the faith which has gone hand-in-hand with their growth in other areas of knowledge and experience. These crises are the result of under-developed religious knowledge.

I don't think you can argue that lectures on religion and theology at the university are an adequate counterweight. Quite apart from their effectiveness (if they have any) it is not the classes themselves that need underlining (in some universities, at least, they have changed a great deal in format and content) but the *attitude* of those who attend them. Revelation is not a philosophy. It is not something which should be learned as just another subject. Either you try to live it or you completely fail to understand it. In other words you cannot get a deeper understanding of the Gospel unless you are prepared to practise it in your own personal life. If this does not happen (as is very common), religion — one's relationship with God born from faith in revelation — is completely separated from life; it has no influence on life. Perhaps certain practices remain but these eventually become empty of meaning and even lose their basis. Piety, then, is purely external and gives way to pharisaism. And then, since the young student finds pharisaism repellent, and his knowledge of the faith is superficial and inadequate, he decides to 'be genuine' and give up the practice of his faith. He even stops thinking about these things. The enthusiasm with which a person like this adopts humanitarian ideals, taking up the fight against poverty, injustice, hunger or war in a kind of philanthropic and altruistic crusade is partly (at least in some cases) a kind of substitute for the faith he has given up, if not lost. The thing gets worse when someone feels he is now freed of his bonds and devotes himself to living according to the flesh, smothering the spirit. And it is very difficult to find any cure when you set up your own intelligence in the centre of things and make your own ideas the criteria of truth. In your blindness you are capable of even putting the blame on God rather than admitting your own mistakes, your obvious limitations and your evident carelessness.

Unconverted minds

Perhaps I'm not expressing myself well. What I mean is this: we are on the receiving end of a continuous barrage of ideas which reach us through the papers, radio, television, articles, novels, films, theatre, books, social behaviour, the environment we live in — just like a skin-diver, who feels the pressure of the water on all sides. Alright: generally all these ideas which reach us, or at least the great majority of them, not only do not lead us to God (unless by way of exception and through pure reaction) but rather tend to keep us from him. Faced with this barrage, what defence does the faith normally have? A mind which is constantly being fed with ideas, concepts and criteria which have no reference to the Gospel or go against it: what chance has it of remaining loyal to the faith of Christ, if it starts out with almost no knowledge of that faith?

In fact, I think that it would not be difficult to find, in Catholics with non-Catholic minds: that is, Catholics whose thinking on many subjects is either not in agreement with or directly contrary to the faith which they openly hold or at least have never explicitly denied. I daresay that Ronald Knox was getting at this (at least I think it was Knox) when he said that a non-intellectual conversion often meant an unconverted mind. But, in this case, what hope is there for the world if those who should save it, have, through their ignorance of the saving doctrine, rendered themselves unable to do so, since they themselves have not yet saved their own minds?

Acquiring an adequate knowledge of the faith

Except through a special grace from God it is not possible to love him with all your mind if you do not take steps to develop your mind in matters connected with revealed truth. And you will not get a better grasp of revealed truth unless you learn it, unless you work at it. It is not something you can make up by yourself, no matter how intelligent, intuitive and sensitive you are. Therefore, the development of your mind in order to get an adequate knowledge of the faith (adequate to your intellectual development and on par with your secular knowledge) should be sought through reading.

It might be useful at this point to recall that St Teresa of Avila noticed she had a strong and almost instinctive tendency not to read religious books unless they were 'very approved'. To our modern minds this of course rings of censorship, limitation of freedom and narrowmindedness. Personally, I don't think St Teresa was like that; she quite simply did not want to be taken in.

I quote her here because I have the impression that the university student is more inclined to read an essay that is easy and not too deep than a book which contains sound doctrine but which is not really entertaining. And I would not dare suggest that possibly some young university people only read books which are topical and fashionable, not caring whether their content is true, or their arguments well founded. And I don't want even to think that some of you might want to read only those books which back up your own hard opinions.

You cannot love what you do not know. Can you know Jesus without knowing the Gospel? How many times has the average university man or woman — you can average them from the oldest professor to the freshman — read the four Gospels? How many of them have read them *in their entirety* even once? Of course, I don't know. But sometimes I wonder whether this ignorance of essential matters is not the reason why there are university people and intellectuals (whether a few or many, I don't know) whose idea of Christ, the Gospel and the Church is so rudimentary and deformed that, when it comes to committing themselves, they go overboard about any ideology, any one, rather than about the faith in which they were baptised.

Advice: read the faith every day

If you were to ask my advice this is what I would say: every day spend some time reading a book which acts as daily nourishment for the mind. Not any book but suitable books; books which meet at least these two requirements – sound doctrine (this is the same as saying that it is in keeping with the teaching of the Church) and intelligibility (it is suited to the intelligence and training of the reader). It may seem unnecessary to argue the reason for these two requirements, but anyway I'm going to do just that. If a person wants to learn physics he does not go to Jules Verne or some modern science-fiction writer. He looks for books written by physicists, preferably by physicists in good standing. That's just common sense. Well then, if someone wants to get a deeper understanding of his faith or simply a better knowledge of the Gospel and he takes up articles on theology-fiction or religious sociology, he is being very clever; not only will he not increase his knowledge but he is liable to mess up the little knowledge he had when he started. As regards the second requirement, you need only remember what we were saying about the geometry textbook for the twelve-year-old and the fourth year maths student.

'You shall love the Lord your God with all your mind'. An adequate knowledge of the faith which is at least on par with your secular knowledge is not a luxury. It is an obligation not limited to those ivory tower people who look down on events as sheer dirt: it applies to every Christian, no matter how busy he is, no matter how big the job he's holding down. A few minutes is not a lot of time, anyway, but it can be enough.

Because the Church is the mystical Body of Christ, we are members of a Body. Our weakness, carelessness and mediocrity are doing real harm to the whole Church: that is, we are harming all the other members. Do you still think God is being too demanding when he asks us to love him also with our whole mind?

I know that you are free and that you can do it or not do it. It's your business. But don't forget that, precisely because you are free, you have to answer for what you do . . . and what you fail to do. The use of the gift of freedom, which has been given you so that you can love, involves supreme responsibility before God. The Judgement of God or the particular judgement is no theory; it is not something we can choose or reject. It is an event which we all have to confront as soon as death appears on the scene.

Do you also wish to go away?

Of the four evangelists, St John, according to the experts, is strongest on chronology: he is the one who keeps closest to the order of events in our Lord's life. Perhaps this is why, when you read his Gospel, you get a rather dramatic impression of a gradual, steady change in the atmosphere around Jesus — starting with the enthusiasm of the first few months of his public life and ending with the total desolation of the cross.

Our Lord's public life, those three years which he devoted to proclaiming the Good News, develops in a rather dramatic way. At first, the people receive him enthusiastically; the religious authorities are well-disposed (for centuries there had been no prophet in Israel); the Sadducees are probably rather indifferent (they did not believe in much and they liked to live well) and the Pharisees are probably a little reserved. Our Lord moved quite freely, followed by eager crowds who even wanted to make him king. Then you find that very, very gradually, whereas the people stay the same, the attitudes of the Sanhedrin, the Pharisees and the Sadducees begin to change — especially because the people tended, almost without realizing it, to make comparisons and Jesus spoke 'not like the scribes and the Pharisees, but as one who had authority'; and as if that were not enough, the moment came when our Lord began to denounce the way the Pharisees had falsified religion. To ask them, on top of this, to take it all calmly was going a bit too far.

Our Lord never yielded in matters of truth for tactical reasons; thus, his various encounters and discussions with the rulers of the Jews became more and more frequent and sometimes very difficult. The people began to notice this growing opposition and although his prestige among them was not affected and they still crowded to listen to him, they could not but be influenced by the obvious reserve shown by the scribes and Pharisees — especially when the Sanhedrin decided to debar from the synagogue those who followed him. His popularity began to fall off the more the Pharisees moved among the people to undermine it; sooner or later a crisis point would come.

At one particular moment, the situation underwent a change — a subtle change perhaps, yet one you can notice from the Gospel. Jesus could not go to Jerusalem because 'the Jews were seeking to put him to death.' The religious leaders of the Jewish people were so impatient that at one stage they sent men to arrest him. They did not in fact arrest him: they found him surrounded by a crowd and they waited for him to finish in case they caused an uproar; when he did finish they were so struck by his words that they forgot about the orders they had received. And when they went back and were asked, 'Why did you not bring him?,' all they could reply was, 'Never has man spoken as this man' (Jn 7:46). The Gospels give the impression that toward the end of his preaching, the religious authorities were making things very uncomfortable for our Lord; he went from place to place as if he were being followed and harrassed, and, more than once, he had to go into the desert or to the other side of Jordan, or cross the border into Gentile country.

Jesus' message was this: I am the Messiah; I am the one sent by God to save men, as he promised centuries ago. And the Jews replied: You are a liar; you are an impostor who has deceived the people. Our Lord would say: If you do not believe in what I say, then at least believe in what I do (and he raised the dead, gave sight to the blind, healed lepers, fed a crowd of over five thousand using only a few fish and some loaves of bread, made the deaf hear, the dumb speak and the lame walk). But the Jews, becoming rather fanatical, replied: Don't believe him. If he did miracles, it wasn't by God's power but by the power of Beelzebub, the prince of devils. He is possessed.

This is the general impression one gets from reading St John's Gospel (well, I must admit it comes from years of reading it); and I thought it useful to run through it so you can see the context, the general setting of one particular event in our Lord's life which I want you to look at today.

I do not want to go through the details of the actual event itself, the actual critical moment: if you are curious or interested you can read this for yourself in St John, chapter six.

The event

The fact is that after the address on the Eucharist, which Jesus gave in the Capharnaum synagogue, things did not go on normally. This time the people — as they left the synagogue — gathered in small groups discussing what they had just heard. You know the sort of things when something happens in college; instead of going home after lectures, you hang around in the hall in little groups, moving from group to group, commenting and giving your views; I think you all know that typical atmosphere of vague uneasiness and tension — and a tendency to get enthusiastic when someone plays the right tune or organizes a compact group which knows what it wants and takes the initiative.

Well, what St John says in this passage gives me that kind of impression. This proved to be — so it seems — the occasion when the tension between our Lord and the Jews reached a crisis point; and you get the feeling that Jesus did not really try to avoid it; it is as if he welcomed a situation which would get rid of vagueness or uncertainty. On the level of doctrine, he went for maximum clarity; as far as people were concerned, he did not put out the wick which still smouldered but he wanted to make it quite clear that he who did not gather with him was in fact scattering.

So, when Jesus came out of the synagogue, he met this atmosphere of discontent and complaint; as he passed by one group he heard the remark, 'This is a hard saying. Who can listen to it?' Naturally, given the way things were, a false step could have precipitated a very serious situation: a minimum of human prudence seemed called for, a conciliatory attitude on Jesus' part. He should now refine certain points and put them another way: perhaps he had spoken somewhat too bluntly for the Jews' taste. He should now try to take the heat out of the situation. But then you read the Gospel and, to your surprise, instead of adopting this sort of line, Jesus is much more impolitic; he stops to address the group that made this remark; he forces the issue and makes them say what they mean: 'Does this scandalize you? What then if you should see the Son of Man ascending where he was before?'

St John, who was present, notes in his Gospel the result of this incident: 'From this time, many of his disciples turned back and no longer went about with him' (Jn 6:66).

For or against

I don't think that either Jesus' sermon or what he said to those who were complaining was what *caused* all these followers to leave him. Rather, I think that it was the excuse they needed for deserting him without feeling bad about it. Now that the religious authorities had openly shown they were opposed to him; now that the Pharisees and the Sadducees, the two largest and most influential groups in the country, had joined forces with the Sanhedrin, following our Lord was less than comfortable and those who had followed him did not want to compromise themselves and risk getting hurt. That is not to say that they now sided with the Pharisees; they probably still were sympathetic to Jesus but they wanted to avoid complications: they wanted to be officially neutral.

As soon as Jesus and the twelve disciples were alone, our Lord again surprises us with his take-it-or-leave-it attitude. Instead of raising their spirits and boosting their morale by telling them it was all for the best (just as well those people had gone off, they were really in the way, etc.); instead of doing that, he turned to them and put their backs against the wall: 'Do you also wish to go away?' Without giving any kind of explanation for his sermon, he asks them also to say where they stand. Either they believe in him and, because they believe in him, they stand by him; or else they do not believe in him — in which case, it is better if they go away. As on another memorable occasion, it was Peter who took the initiative and said what had to be said: 'Lord, to whom shall we go? You have words of everlasting life and we have come to believe and to know that you are the Christ, the Son of God.'

Living faith

So, the twelve disciples stayed. Why did they stay while the rest of his followers left? If our Lord had words of everlasting life, he had them as much for one group as the other and, as for the believing that he was the Christ, . . . did Judas, who also stayed, believe it? Surely some of those who went away out of cowardice rather than lack of faith must have believed it? Anyway, it seems that believing was not enough; you also had to maintain, defend and express this belief when the need arose; you had to have a *living* faith, a faith which influenced not just an isolated decision but all the acts of your life.

I don't know if you have ever thought about this part of the

Gospel. It is important, perhaps particularly because in the university this sort of thing happens so often that you hardly notice it. Not that there are students who openly deny Christ (of course, there may be); but then these Jews did not deny him openly; they limited themselves, as St John tells us, to not going around with him. They simply left him.

So you see, I do think that a number of you have the same attitude (perhaps more than you'd think, since practically all of you are Catholics). Of course you do not deny Jesus Christ; you are far from denying him formally. That would be apostasy. You don't deny him; all you do is stop following him, because walking along with him means that you must believe in him more than in others, put more faith in what he says than in what others say and even what you yourselves think; following him means committing your whole life, your whole personality, in such a way that there is no room for compromise or ambiguity: you are either with him or against him. It means preferring him to many other things which strongly attract us and which we are unable, or do not dare, or do not want, to give up.

Don't blame others

For some time now, teachers, parents and priests involved in the university 'apostolate' have been concerned about the increasing coldness to religion found among students (oddly enough, the group which has more and better opportunities to really get a deep knowledge of the Faith). I think this coldness to religion *is* a fact; and I think that university students today are much more closed than twenty years ago to the Church's teaching (on faith and morals, doctrine and norms of conduct taken from the Gospel); whereas, on the other hand, they are much more credulous; they absorb much more easily all kinds of ideas and theories which dismiss the Gospel and support what are referred to nowadays (if I am not mistaken) as the suppression of 'taboos' and situation ethics.

Why is this phenomenon ('Many no longer went about with him') evident to anyone who looks at you and takes an interest in you? The blame has been put on the parents, on schools, on the way religion has been taught over the years. Never on yourselves (at least not in books, magazines and newspapers). And yet, I would ask, why do you find the same things, often, among older people, in your parents, in your university teachers, in many people who are no longer young? Is it also the fault of *their* parents, the school *they* went to, the teachers *they* had? Those who left our Lord after his sermon in Capharnaum on the Eucharist: did they leave him because he wasn't teaching the Gospel properly or because their parents had not trained them properly? Why did only a few disciples stay behind, whiie the majority went away?

Naturally, I cannot give you the absolute explanation — which only God and themselves know. But I can tell you something which has helped me more than once; it may also be of help to you, if you want to listen.

Personal friendship

During his public life, our Lord covered the whole of Palestine. He went through the towns and villages preaching the kingdom of heaven, and many people gathered to hear him; crowds, amazed and enthusiastic, benefited from the miracles he worked. However, a small number of his disciples (not as enthusiastic as you might think) stayed with him the whole time; they spoke to him, had their meals with him, asked him questions and chatted with him about everyday occurrences and about important questions. In other words, they were in close contact with him. Do you see where this is leading us? Those who had daily contact with our Lord and were his personal friends stayed loyal to him. Those who listened to him and followed his occasionally or at least did not have this personal relationship with him, those who were duly amazed and enthusiastic but had no personal bond of friendship with Jesus, as soon as they saw that things might not go smoothly, ceased to go around with him.

I don't know exactly how to put it to you to make you realize what I am trying to say. Personal contact leads to friendship and, when this friendship is mutual, sincere and deep, you trust your friend, for if friendship is genuine it is always refined: there is no abuse or deception. I am referring, of course, to *personal* friendship. Not to that superficial kind of friendship among people who share a few interests, ideas or aims — a friendship which stems from those aims, ideas or interests and not from the persons themselves, a friendship which disappears as soon as they cease to share these things. No, I am talking about the friendship between two people which is independent of anything other than what is purely personal. When you have that kind of friendship, you also get a sense of loyalty. And that, I think, is what happened on the occasion in question. Only ·those disciples of Christ who, through daily contact, had personal friendship with him, were loyal to him; for they *believed* in him; they knew him very well and the links which bound them to him were very strong. Not even Judas left him at this time.

I ask myself how many of you, of those of you who have given up following him, or who may at some stage give up: how many of you have had a *personal* friendship with our Lord. Don't deceive yourselves. Friendship calls for knowledge and contact, and it is very difficult to be friends with a person (I refer to friendship, not just a vague liking: they are two different things) whose company you do not cultivate. Cultivating Christ's company does not mean reciting some pious formula now and again or making an occasional request (some very personal request, to do with some very worldly object) — particularly when you have only the vaguest idea of who Christ is anyway.

Christ, a living person

Jesus Christ is a person; in fact he is the Son of God. And he is not a pure spirit; he is God and Man; he is a perfect man. And he is alive; he sees us and hears us and is able to speak to us, even though by way of forming his words inside our minds. I am talking about speaking to him, as one friend to another, every day; not with formulas but spontaneously; not on artificial subjects but about the little things of everyday, your concerns, unimportant events and the work you do; speaking to him every day just as his disciples did, just as we do to other people.

In other words, I am referring to prayer, which is the name we give to conversation with God. For without prayer (whatever be the form it takes), there is no contact and, without contact, there is no friendship. And if there is no prayer, that is, if that friendly relationship with our Lord is missing, how is it possible to get to know him, to understand his words, to appreciate the sacraments — in a word to *believe* in him? Don't you understand why so many things which you learned as children seem unintelligible to you now? Why should one bother about the words of one he hardly knows? Why should he be loyal to someone whom he has hardly any relationship with?

I know that this is not a defect which is somehow peculiar to you. I think it is general. Nowadays there is the belief, among many practising Catholics, that prayer is something for monks and nuns (at least the kind we used to see); as far as the small little world of the university is concerned, I feel that for many people, on all levels, prayer is something completely outside their range of interests.

And yet, without prayer, you can have no communication with God (at least, normally that is the case). And without communication, is it possible for our Lord to be anything for us other than a vague idea or a confused image? Is it possible to *love* such a vague idea or image to the extreme of total loyalty? No wonder the Jews, or so many of them, stopped following him. In the same way it is not surprising, it is quite logical, to find that steady dechristianization, that progressive shedding of Christianity that is taking place in the western world — the world which people still describe as 'Christian' in spite of everything.

I think that if most of us leave a lot to be desired as Catholics, if we are a stumbling block, if we are inconsistent, easy-going and wavering, or merely performers of pious practices; if we give the impression that following Christ is a matter simply or essentially of being morally rigorous, keeping to the letter of the Law and getting lost in casuistry like the Pharisees, or of going to Mass and believing theoretically in a whole heap of things we never think about, so that our life follows a course which contradicts the Faith we publicly claim to hold; if there is a steadily increasing number of people who stop following Christ, if that sort of thing is the order of the day, it is because we are not men of prayer; we have no personal link with Christ, no close relationship with him, no personal loyalty to him. The external cult of our religion is no longer implemented by interior life; and so easily appears unauthentic and artificial to many.

This holds true for everyone — even for you and me and my colleagues. I think it is increasingly difficult to keep oneself on a loose rein; just as the tension between our Lord and the Jews reached the point of crisis, we too find ourselves in a critical time when we all have to say where we stand. And, just as then, I think it is very unlikely that we shall be able to stay loyal to Christ if we have no relationship or friendship with him. That is, unless for reasons known only to him, some are able to get along without having to face such crisis.

'Lord, to whom shall we go? You have words of everlasting life; and we have come to believe and to know that you are the Christ, the Son of God.' And they stayed. Who else could they go to? Friendship and knowledge had united them to him in such a way that, without him, they did not know where to go or who to go to. Without him they were alone, helpless and lost. In an inverse way St Augustine had the same kind of experience: his life was all restlessness until he found peace in Christ.

I pray to God to give you light and strength to stay loyal to him should the need arise and you have to take a stand. But if you are not men of prayer, I think it is as difficult to achieve this loyalty as it is for someone to survive without food.

The first stone

The scribes and Pharisees could be praised for their tenacity were it not that they so frequently abused it. The Gospels are sown with snares set for our Lord, sly questions maliciously posed at an appropriate time, aimed at finding some inconsistency; they wanted to find something they could use to make him lose face, or ideally to allow them to indict him and remove him altogether from the scene.

At last they thought they had a really good opportunity. I think you will all remember the episode of the adulterous woman. St John describes it briefly and vividly. Let's get the facts from him first and then think a bit about it.

> And at daybreak he came again into the temple and all the people came to him: and sitting down he began to teach them.
>
> Now the scribes and Pharisees brought a woman caught in adultery and setting her in the midst, said to him, 'Master, this woman has just now been caught in adultery. And in the Law, Moses commanded us to stone such persons. What, therefore, do you say?' Now, they were saying this to test him, in order that they might be able to accuse him. But Jesus, stooping down, began to write with his fingers on the ground.
>
> But when they continued asking him, he raised himself and said to them, 'Let him who is without sin among you be the first to cast a stone at her.' And again stooped down, he began to write on the ground. But hearing this, they went away, one by one, beginning with the eldest (Jn 8:2-9).

So, once more we see our Lord surrounded by people, pressing about him, listening to him. There is hardly any free space — just a little semi-circle so he can have a certain freedom of movement and scope for speaking. There, 'in the midst,' the scribes and Pharisees set this poor woman who had been caught committing adultery; there they put her and expose her to the unhealthy curiosity of the crowd. The whole thing is done to a tee, both as far as the crowd is concerned (it is calculated to attract their attention) and also for Jesus, for the sudden arrival of this strange group and their bringing up this kind of case would be enough to disconcert anyone. In fact, any bystander would think the scribes and Pharisees were submitting an important question to the Master's judgement. The whole thing could be interpreted as a gesture of goodwill, expressing a desire to resolve a genuine doubt. In the Law, Moses had ordered that an adulterous woman should be stoned; but times had changed — fourteen centuries had left their mark; attitudes were different, customs had become more defined. On the other hand, up to what point could one disobey the Law? What was the Master's opinion? What would he advise them to do?

A dilemma

As usual when the Pharisees addressed our Lord, things were not exactly as they appeared at first sight. Even if the Gospel had not exactly shown up their bad intentions ('they were saying this to test him, in order that they might be able to accuse him'), a little reflection would show their 'simple' goodwill was only superficial. If the woman had been caught *in the very act* of adultery, where was the man she had committed it with? The Law of Moses which they were invoking said: 'If a man commits adultery with his neighbor's wife, both the adulterer and the adulteress shall be put to death' (Lv 20:10). Why had they just brought the woman? Moreover, if they wanted to resolve a genuine doubt, if there really was a conflict of conscience and they wanted advice as to their duty in regard to a precept which seemed inhumanly harsh, why were they airing their conflicts of conscience in the public square, surrounded by people who had no interest in their personal, interior problems? Why humiliate the woman, dragging her through the city, shouting her name, exposing her to the unhealthy curiosity of the passers-by, publicizing her fault and exhibiting her as a trophy?

It was all rather suspicious. But people do not generally react to this sort of occurrence by asking questions — particularly when they are taken by surprise and everything happens so fast that they have no time to think. Moreover, the

Pharisees set it up so cleverly that, with one word, they were able to take attention off themselves and focus it on the woman and on Jesus. Their intentions were dishonest and it seems they were not very concerned about the woman's sin — except insofar as they could use it as a weapon against Jesus. We must admit that they played their cards very well: 'In the Law, Moses commanded us to stone such persons. What, therefore, do you say?'

What could he say? He could, for example, follow through on what he had publicly taught about it being not the healthy but the sick who needed a doctor; he could have said that he had not come to seek the just, but, rather, sinners. Or he might have recalled the criteria he had given about not breaking the crushed reed, nor putting out the smouldering wick. In other words, he could have had pity on the poor woman and saved her, maybe so that she could do penance for her sin. Perhaps this was what they expected him to do, what they wanted him to do: this would allow them to accuse him of setting himself against Moses and the Law; and it would show him up as a liar, for he had said he came not to destroy the Law but to bring it to fulfilment. This was a *cul-de-sac*.

Or following it to the letter, he could have abided by the Law, stating that he had no objection to the execution of the sentence given by Moses; he could have declared himself in favour of the sentence. But in this case, what hope could sinners cling to? Was his presence in the world necessary for saying something which had already been said? Had he come to destroy sin or to destroy the sinner? And how, in this case, could such a rigorous attitude fit in with the open call he had made to people to repent and obtain forgiveness.

It did not look as though he could easily get out of this dilemma — and both our Lord and the Pharisees seemed to realize it. In other situations, Jesus gave an immediate answer, leaving his questioners speechless, with no escape. But this time it was he who had nothing to say: 'But Jesus, stooping down, began to write with his finger on the ground'; he seemed to be stalling, like someone looking desperately for a suitable phrase to avoid public ridicule; it seemed as if he were trying to gain time to think of something to say.

Misusing other people

That is how the Pharisees must have interpreted his silence and the way he seemed to be avoiding the question by scribbling on the ground; so they began to harass him. They thought they had him at their mercy, just where they wanted him. Until our Lord had enough of the game: 'But when they continued asking him, he raised himself and said to them, "Let him who is without sin among you be the first to cast a stone on her." And again stooping down, he began to write on the ground.'

Well, had they not been looking for an answer? Now they were satisfied, though I doubt if you could describe as satisfaction their feelings when they heard it. Once again, our Lord's reply was as surprising as it was unexpected. This time, it was not like what happened years before when Mary and Joseph found him, after three days searching, with the doctors in the temple. Then, too, Jesus had replied to a question but 'they did not understand the word that he spoke to them.' Not that it mattered very much; they were content enough to know that there was an answer, even if they did not grasp it at the time.

The scribes and Pharisees certainly did understand our Lord. They understood him so well that none would reach for the first stone and open fire. In silence, they slunk off: ('they went away,' the Gospel tells us), 'one by one, beginning with the eldest.' It was now they who pretended not to understand, who wanted to forget the whole business; it was they who 'went away', with no further explanation, from the situation they themselves had so carefully set up. As long as they thought they had Jesus cornered, they kept at him, pressing him, demanding an answer; the moment he spoke, they suddenly lost all interest in what had brought them there; apparently they now remembered some urgent business which had slipped their minds.

There are people like that. People who attack their adversary before he gets on his feet, people who do not mind landing low punches; they use others as things (not persons) and, naturally, they do not care if they do damage. The Pharisees were just like that. They came to our Lord, pushing the woman in front of them, and spat out their question. Do they give him time to think? No. They demand his answer immediately and, when our Lord appears to be taking his time, they keep at him. Their real objective was quite different from what it seemed to be, though this could not be proved from the way they put their question. They did not care what Moses had said: they were just using it to compromise Jesus. They were concerned not so much with fulfilling the Law as with disqualifying this man whom they considered their enemy. And what about the woman? They were just making use of her. They were not concerned about those they shoved and stepped on, humiliating them or burying them in the process without even noticing it, so intent were they on reaching their objective (this is sometimes called 'effectiveness'). People who put their faith in an idea or a theory and sacrifice everything to attain it: what does it matter, the *real* damage they do, compared with the good they *think* they are going to do once their ideal wins out? People who plan a perfect business, looking after every factor which economics says is important but who do not think of the effects this will have on so many human lives — and of course it would never occur to them to use their surplus wealth to help others. People who make up their own moral laws and use them to justify their personal sins usually corrupt others. People who use arguments about hunger to promote contraceptives; people who fulminate against war, not out of compassion for those who suffer from it but out of hatred for those who are winning; people who continuously clamour for social justice, not because they are concerned about the poor (they have never deprived themselves of any luxury to buy someone a bite to eat) but because they are annoyed that they are not rich themselves. Yes, there are people who, like the Pharisees, have this strange ability to convince themselves to the point of blindness. Today they use big sophisticated words but, very often, they are a cover-up for something that is rotten through and through.

The answer our Lord gives the Pharisees leaves them disinclined to continue this farce. It was a magnificent answer. St Augustine comments as follows: 'How he turned them in on themselves! They were calumniating others but they had not examined themselves; they had seen the adulterous woman but had not looked at themselves. Breakers of the Law, they wanted the Law to be fulfilled, not stopping at calumny to get their own way; they did not condemn her adultery in the name of chastity.' Little did they care about that!

'Let him who is without sin among you be the first to cast a stone at her.' However, the Pharisees this time were sincere enough to accept their humiliation. There was not even one who dared to start the stoning — perhaps because they knew our Lord could read their consciences: it was too dangerous to risk his telling them their own sins in public. Our Lord did not give a judgement on the Law or on the woman. Nor did he judge the Pharisees; all he did was, by a simple remark, to oblige them to take a look at themselves. Obviously, they did not like what they saw, for they left the scene without saying a word — the older ones being the first to go.

Protest is in fashion

Nowadays, a lot of stones are thrown at things human and things divine; there is so much altercation, so many things are protested about, so many defects are denounced, so many faults and mistakes are exposed; the older and younger generations are at loggerheads; children claim their parents do not understand them and parents are bemused by their children: they think they have gone off their heads with strange ideas which they cannot understand and which (they feel) are subversive and stupid. This whole situation, to my mind, is largely due to our general distaste, nowadays, for getting inside ourselves, taking a good look at ourselves, at what's going on inside us. We are so taken up with judging other people, heaping blame on other people, that we have no time for taking a good hard look at our own behaviour. Let's put it bluntly: we simply refuse to see and acknowledge our own sins, our own mistakes, our own faults, our own lies, our own untruthfulness.

Like the Pharisees, we are so convinced that we are in the right that we blame and condemn other people. We are so sure of the rightness of our position that we are unable to see the damage we do all round us, precisely to innocent people who really are not responsible for things not being to our taste. Of course, we never think that maybe we ourselves are not *completely* right, that perhaps we *may* be mistaken, at least to some extent.

The value of reflection

This civilisation in which we are living, in the midst of many wonderful things which are the result of a whole series of patient contributions, sifted and perfected over many generations, is not characterized by that 'composure' which encourages reflection. It is not a civilization which makes interiority easy; in fact, I would go as far as to say that, taken as a whole, it is a civilization which uses very powerful means to break down interiority. It fights interiority through pressure to hurry, through productivity (I hope you know what I mean), through the mass media, through speed, superficiality and even technology. And it has produced a kind of man who no longer reflects but rather feeds on news and clichés, either because he has already become a robot specialized in some particular kind of work or simply because he has no free time, no real leisure and even no taste for interiority.

'Let him who is without sin among you be the first to cast a stone at her.' Fewer people would throw stones if they concentrated more on their interior life; maybe then, when they see the huge plank in their own eye, they would not focus so much on the speck they see in their brother's. It is not that we are blind to ourselves, I think; it is simply that we don't look.

God forbid that I should throw a stone at you, at your attitudes and your motives. I am not so free from sin as that; I am sure that the plank in my eye is bigger than the speck in yours. Years ago I read these words: 'It's easier said than done. With that cutting, hatchet-like tongue, have you ever tried, even by chance, to do "well" what, according to your "considered" opinion, others do less well?' (J. Escrivá, *The Way*, 448).

I cannot, I do not wish to judge you (on what grounds, in whose name could I do it?); but certainly I would like to make you think, if I possibly can. I would like you to look inside yourselves with a calmness which creates a certain composure. I do not want you to convince yourselves that your course is right; I want you to check whether you really are as pure as the Pharisees thought they were before our Lord gave them something to think about. There are too many good things in you for you just to throw them out the window, letting yourselves be caught in the trap which today's over-developed society has so cleverly laid: living for the outside, not for the inside; substituting advertising for thought, television for reading, noise for silence, exhibitionism for privacy, news and catch-phrases for ideas; judging others but never, never judging yourself; blaming your neighbour but doing everything you can to avoid examining your own interior world, in case you have to accuse yourself because you find you are as dirty as the society you are condemning.

And if after taking a good look at yourself, with that sincerity which they say is a feature of youth, if you find you are pure and without sin, then stir yourself and get on with the job. You can throw the first stone, because you have seen that our Lord authorizes it. But if you find that you too are a sinner and you see planks in your own eye, then it is better for you to move away in silence. For if you persist in condemning other people, then you are being as hypocritical as any Pharisee.

But if after leaving the scene, in the silence of truthful reflection, you are man enough to acknowledge your own mistakes and your own failings, and if you go on to correct yourself and start again, then you will have won the game. You may become a somewhat less enthusiastic type but you will certainly be a humbler person and that is a much surer basis for doing well what you have to do. And maybe, if you act in this way, you will then be able to help others to take the specks out of their eyes because you have already gotten rid of the plank that was in your own.

They did not believe in him

'Now though he had worked so many signs in their presence, they did not believe in him' (Jn 12:37). When you read these words, or better still, when you reflect on them, you get the impression that the disciples were perplexed by this amazing unbelief. In a preceding chapter, St John gives a detailed report of the resurrection of Lazarus. This was an event which had wide repercussions, but surprisingly enough, it also gave rise to adverse reactions. Overwhelmed by the miracle, many of the Jews who witnessed it 'believed in him,' says St John. Others, however, went to report it to the Pharisees who, together with the chief priests, felt impelled to take decisive action when they heard what had happened: 'What are we doing? For this man is working many signs.' They decided to kill him because ' "if we leave him alone as he is all will believe in him." So from that day forth, their plan was to put him to death' (Jn 11:45f).

Lazarus was dead, buried for four days, his corpse reeking from decomposition. Jesus arrived, gave an order to the dead man, and Lazarus emerged alive and healthy from the grave. How was it possible — the disciples asked themselves, totally disconcerted, perplexed and amazed — that there could be Jews who did not believe in the face of such prodigious miracles? And yet, St John says clearly, 'now though he had worked so many signs in their presence, they did not believe in him'.

But why? What else could Jesus do? What else did he have to do to convince them of the truth of his words? He gave sight to people blind from birth: he gave back speech to the dumb; he made the lame walk, cured the lepers of their rotten flesh, commanded the elements to obey him with one simple word. All this had not been sufficient for many Jews. His countrymen continued not believing that he it was who was to come. Was it necessary, then, to go even further? Well, then, he would go further: he would show them that he was Lord over life and death. And this is what he did in the case of Lazarus; one word of command which was obeyed instantly.

The refusal of belief

It was still in vain. Not only did they refuse to believe him; they also made up their minds to kill him.

On one occasion, the Jews asked him, 'What sign, then, do you do, that we may see and believe you? What work do you perform?' They asked this right after Jesus had fed a multitude of five thousand men with just five barley loaves and two fishes. Perhaps this was not a big enough miracle for them; perhaps they wanted to see something of a different order. They never specified. Anyway, could they have thought of any miracle better than the resurrection of Lazarus who already began to stink? Could there be anything more conclusive, more definitive? The fact remains that they still did not believe in him even after the many miracles he performed. Yet after this last proof of his divinity, it was no longer possible to maintain the facade of being people who do not want to be credulous and who ask for proofs on which to stand. After this last resistance after this last voluntary hardness, they could not ask for more. There were more than enough proofs to take the leap of faith and they were under pressure to take up a final option. Were they to bow their heads, acknowledge their obstinacy and have faith in him? Could they still oppose the testimony of Jesus ('The works that I do in the name of my Father, these bear witness concerning me')? Could they offer any argument, have any reservations, any reasonable doubt? It doesn't seem so, judging from their reaction. But in that case, why did they not believe him?

Whatever the answer, it is difficult to unravel the profound mystery that surrounds the attitude of a free man facing God's demands. But from the moment man is what he is — namely, an intelligent, free being — we can reasonably affirm that among the impediments hindering him from accepting the faith is simply his not wanting to. This refusal can reach the extreme limit of hatred, as expressed by the Pharisees and chief priests after the resurrection of Lazarus. And I do not doubt that, nowadays as always, there are cases in which the attitude toward Christ is very similar. Diabolical activity — the devil is the 'prince of this world' — is a fact, even if some people think it a fable. Clearly, there is no need for everyone to have personal experience of the devil but neither is there any reason why lack of such personal experience should be an argument against the devil's existence and doings.

However, without going to that extreme, the breakdown of faith is so obvious a phenomenon in today's world that even the blind can see it. Theories abound which attempt to explain it and many discuss the matter seriously, tenaciously, insistently and even obsessively. In general, the initiative along these lines (so it seems to non-specialists) came from Protestant theologians of various denominations. On such initiative, the so-called 'theology of the death of God,' seems to have dazzled even some Catholics (mostly ecclesiastics) who were completely taken in by the spectacular publicity it got in the popular press and easily swallowed the unfounded, heretical arguments put forward. Thus, the figure of the Good Atheist has emerged: a typical twentieth century version of the eighteenth century 'freethinker'; a sincere man who meets problems on a profound intellectual level, who asks himself honestly about God, the meaning of life, the existence of evil, injustice and violence. A curious kind of lay saint who searches and searches and constantly reflects on the reality of things . . .

The image of the modern atheist

Formerly, the atheist was presented as someone who, lacking belief in God, Christ and the life hereafter, lived in utter moral depravity without any reason to subject his life to ethical norms — a hypocrite whose atheism was a mere pretext for not adhering to a moral code, although, deep down inside, he was convinced about God, Christ and the life hereafter. Today, the direction of the wind has changed; it blows from the opposite extreme. The atheist is the honest, open, sincere man who sees himself obliged to reject God and the world of grace out of strict intellectual honesty. On the other hand, the hypocrite (at least this is the impression one gets from some articles which steadily grow in number and which become more and more superficial) is he who believes without more ado, without questioning his faith, without criticising what he was taught, without protesting against injustice, war and hunger: in short, an insincere man who accepts faith and the established order hook-line-and-sinker, without bothering to look around him and getting involved in the world, its development and maturity. Without fear of exaggeration, I believe that atheism is somehow the 'in thing' nowadays. It seems as if denying truths whose profession is obligatory for any Catholic to remain Catholic (the divinity of Jesus, the Church, the virginity of Mary, the sacraments) is a sign of sincerity, authenticity and intellectual honesty. (Although this may be true in some cases, it does not substantiate in any way the arguments of those who go back on their faith.)

Freedom and the act of faith

Basically (and acknowledging the mysterious nature of the act of faith) faith has mainly to do with our willingness to respond to God's grace. If the Jews (the religious and civil authorities of the country, the scribes, the Pharisees, etc.) did not believe in Jesus in spite of the miracles he performed in their midst, it was because faith is not an act we are compelled to make: it is a free act. It is not, as Newman reminded us, the necessary conclusion of some premises; there is no faith at all when one accepts the proposition 'Two plus two equals four,' 'The whole is larger than any of its parts,' and other similar assertions. Naturally, assent to these propositions is not a free act or a matter of choice: they are truths spontaneously 'imposed,' as it were, on the intellect. It is possible, J. Pieper tells us, that the credibility of a man is made manifest to me in so convincing a way that I cannot but say, 'I have to believe him.' However, this last step can only be taken in complete freedom, which means that it could also be withheld. There can be many convincing arguments which lead us to believe that a man is worthy of our faith or not, but no argument can force us to believe him. The unanimity of opinions on this point is astounding, all the way down from St Augustine and St Thomas, to Kierkegaard, Newman and Gide.

I feel that a good example of the truth of this observation is given by the Jews during our Lord's time and by the good atheists of today. Jesus gave all possible proof that he was a person deserving complete belief. Greater proofs than those he gave are impossible. Why then did they refuse to believe in spite of all his miracles?

Faith is an intellectual act, but it is not merely intellectual. It is intellectual in the sense that it is an assent to what is said by another person (by Christ in this case). It is intellectual also in the sense that it is based on grounds which the intellect deems sufficient testimony to the credibility of the person believed. But faith demands, in addition, an act of the will, since the content of what is believed is not evident in itself. And this act of the will, in accepting or denying faith, can be influenced by a host of factors not strictly logical and reasonable. Especially after the resurrection of Lazarus, the Jews had no reason to refuse belief in Jesus; but they decided to kill him. They had their own ideas, and the revelation which Jesus brought, and of which he gave complete testimony, was destroying that idea. The dilemma was whether to abandon their ideas and believe in Jesus or to kill Jesus who was destroying their ideas.

What prevents people believing

We can learn a lot from the attitude of the Jews. They made their opinions and convictions touchstones with which to assay any other affirmation: it was true in so far as it coincided with what they had in mind; it was false and worthy of derision whenever it did not. The Messianic revelation Jesus made known did not agree with their views (views which entailed having to ignore things the prophets said which did not tally with their preconceived ideas). Therefore, his works were false and destructive; and because he did not correct himself or subject himself to their ideas, he should be suppressed. They did not admit *at all* the possibility of *their* being wrong; their will rejected everything which did not conform with the attitude they had built around themselves. This decision, truly blind and fanatical, dragged them to the extreme of commiting deicide.

What prevents people believing nowadays? It certainly seems that, for modern man, miracles are absolutely meaningless. He is more prone to believe theories than miracles, apparently. Feuerbach, for example, wrote that it was not God who created man, but rather man who created God by projecting his highest aspirations on to an ideal being (which has, therefore, no existence in reality). He concludes that God is nothing but the ideal image of man alienated from himself. It is true that Feuerbach did not give any proof to substantiate his idea; but this did not stop great hoards of people from being alienated by his theory: given a choice between the resurrection of Lazarus and the affirmation of that disciple of Hegel — that is, between a fact and a theory — they opted passionately for the theory.

The glorification of man has reached almost astronomical

proportions in this present world. Man has achieved, through his intelligence, labour, skill, patience and dedication, amazing feats in the sciences: in biology, in physics, in chemistry. The technological advances are impressive. Who would dare talk of miracles in these heights of glory? And today, perhaps as never before, man has made of his own intelligence the measure of everything, even of God himself. 'What's all this nonsense about the Commandments of God?', modern man asks. *Thou shalt not kill* is acceptable; we agree' (modern man wants nothing of violence; he clamors for the abolition of the death penalty; children, he also maintains, should be spared from corporal punishment, as this may have traumatic effects on the subconscious and later breed violence in them); 'but who said anything about fornication? What's wrong with it anyway? It's simply an old taboo which must be demolished.' (Thus, children are given sex education in a matter of fact way from their early years. Sexual release is encouraged for therapeutic reasons; erotic experiences are considered healthy and worthy of being fostered. 'Eroticism' is distinguished carefully from 'pornography,' while contraceptives are recommended and abortion authorized. Censorship would undermine the art of the film and no novel becomes a best-seller without a suitable dose of sex. The theatre, too, needs erotic scenes . . .)

Man today has made himself the measure of all things and denies everything contrary to his own thinking. Mankind has never looked as depressing as it does today: people with only two dimensions, without depth, without transcendence, who know the why's and the how's of everything, but who are incapable of finding meaning in anything.

Progress: or regression?

The Jews crucified Jesus. In today's world, the death of God has been decreed. The world has come of age, it is scientific; it has shed the credulity of the past. In the last thirty years, progress has posted gains which far exceed the record of the last thirty centuries. And a group of well-meaning theologians, feeling depressed over this situation, have begun to write to each other, analyzing, so to speak, the tenor of the times. Our contemporary godless society has graciously accepted their diagnosis and now orchestrates the theology of the death of God, to help God die a happy death. Today's adult world does not need God at all. It has science which explains everything and technology which provides everything. A god who imposes laws and distributes responsibilities: who needs him? Man can now make his own laws, including a few things from that good chap, that great but impractical idealist called Jesus Christ.

Is this progress? It looks more like regression. It is an attitude very similar to that of the Jews who, despite 'many signs (Jesus did) in their presence . . . did not believe in him.' This cannot be progress at all. If there now exists a growing climate of atheism, it is due, in the first place, to an attitude, not to some reasoning process. Today's man, the atheist of today, and those on the road to losing the faith granted to them as a gift, do not stop to consider whether or not the miracles of Jesus bear sufficient testimony of who he is. They have decided that miracles are mere myths and so they dismiss the problem altogether. 'The resurrection of a dead man?', they ask. 'Well, we also know of reanimated hearts which had stopped beating but which were later revived. Who knows what science will eventually bring?'

And, really, who knows what science will bring? But ask yourself: What has this got to do with faith in Jesus Christ? What kind of argument is this, justifying the lack of faith with a semblance of logic? Faith is not a conclusion of some premises nor is it a consoling inner sentiment. And science, by limiting itself voluntarily to a very restricted area, deliberately ignores everything that does not fall within its scope or object of study.

Faith calls for a certain integrity

Before one can assent to the words of a witness (and faith is assent to the word of God as revealed by Christ), it is first necessary to set aside our prejudices in order to honestly face the facts. The Jews had decided that Jesus was possessed and not even a reality as visible as the resurrection of Lazarus could change their closed minds, although it could (and did) harden them. Similarly, the materialistic outlook of our times has decided that the supernatural is a myth and this *a priori* dogmatism which bars the road to faith is incapable of opening itself even to demonstrated facts.

Peter Wust explains that belief calls for a certain degree of moral integrity. It is the will that moves the intellect to assent to truths not evident in themselves. Hence when the will is conditioned in a certain way, it bears upon the intellect to abide by the prejudice which rationalizes the evil it clings to; or worse, the will moves the intellect to construct ideologies which justify its perverted attitudes, desires and interests. This fact is evident to anyone who reflects on it for a moment: we all tend instinctively to believe whatever suits us best and to go after what is more pleasant. And the acceptance of Christ (who is God-made-man) entails consequences too difficult for those who place their happiness in the acquisition, possession and enjoyment of worldly goods. Those who adore money, sex and power cannot recognize a God whom they do not wish to serve.

The motives behind the incredulity of the Jews were clearly ignoble: 'This man is working many signs. If we let him alone as he is, all will believe in him and the Romans will come and take away both our place and our nation' (Jn 11:48). They were fighting to retain the *status quo;* whether or not Jesus was the Messiah hardly meant anything: what really mattered was that vested interests were protected.

To a dead man everything is dead: the world, thought, other people, trees — everything.   But the world, other people, thought and everything else keep on living when he is nothing but a corpse. The death of God? Would it not be more proper to say that it is we who are dead?

You will not have life in you

In the sixth chapter of St John's gospel we find Jesus' discourse at Caphernaum on the Eucharist — the speech which gave his listeners so much to talk about and provided most of them with the excuse for leaving him altogether. However, given the detrimental effects of original sin on human nature, which make it difficult for man to savour the things of God, it is not really surprising that this teaching of Jesus sounded preposterous (at least given the interpretation they put on it). We, on the other hand, are so familiar with it from childhood that it doesn't cause us a thought.

God's self-abasement

But when we do think about it, we begin to take things more seriously and we are even a little shocked at our usual superficial attitude to this huge mystery of faith *(mysterium fidei)*. I think that what led me, many years ago now, really to think about the Eucharist was some words in Monsignor Escriva's book *The Way:* not that it led me to start speculating in a new way, independently of the faith I had received — to see if I could discover something; no, what it did was make me reflect in a more personal, calmer way. 'The humility of Jesus: in Bethlehem, in Nazareth, and Calvary. But more humiliation and more self-abasement still in the Sacred Host: more than in the stable, more than in Nazareth, more than on the Cross' (cf. *The Way*, 533). Even though it might seem disrespectful (maybe it was) I got the idea of putting myself in Christ's place and I asked myself whether I would be ready to go so far towards total self-abasement and limitation for the good of those I loved — and the very idea almost made me dizzy.

This is not a silly idea, I assure you. Nor is it some piece of literary fiction — something so beautifully expressed that it doesn't matter if it's true or not. I don't know if young people today are really concerned about religion. I don't mean concerned about the clerical-political or sociological-religious news and arguments and dialogues and whatnot that some of the papers are full of. I mean going deep into the truths of faith — reflecting, in interior silence, on revealed truths.

Think a little. God is infinite, almighty, creator of heaven and earth, of everything that is. The distance between God and man (an exceedingly limited creature, no matter how great he thinks he is) is almost inconceivable — because it's infinite. Thinking about infinity, just like thinking about eternity (though I don't think anyone does that nowadays) is something which causes us to shudder. We are too small to take it all in. Well, God did bridge that distance and lowered himself infinitely to take on mortal flesh, assuming human nature in the Person of the Word. Can you imagine what that means? He who is almighty reduced himself to the infinitely inferior condition of a mere man, with all the dependence and limitation and subjection which human nature involves.

I daresay some of you anyway have read Kafka's *Metamorphosis*. In it the central character wakes up one morning to find he has become a horrible insect — I don't exactly remember which kind. He realises this because his mind is still working: he can think and reason; but he can't make himself understood, he can't communicate with other people, can't express himself like a man, because his scope is limited by the inadequate nature in which he is trapped. And he suffers not only because of this enormous limitation but also because he realises that other people are unaware of it and are going to treat him as they see him. Would we be able, for the sake of those we love, to accept freely and gladly that sort of change?

Of course, it is a completely inadequate comparison for the incarnation of the Son of God — but it does give some idea of the limitations and distances involved. Which one of us would be ready to take on an irrational nature while still retaining his self-consciousness? And yet the distance between man and mere animal is almost nothing, when compared with that bridged by God on becoming man.

And now think about the next step. A man, when all is said and done, has intelligence and will: he can express himself and is capable of knowing and loving and taking initiatives; he is lord of his acts; he can speak and write, he can appreciate beauty. An irrational creature can still move and see and feel and call attention to itself, and hide or display itself. But what about a thing, a lifeless object? After contemplating the humiliating death of a God-man on the cross, you might wonder if any greater humiliation, any greater self-abasement were possible. The Eucharist provides the answer: it is possible.

Transubstantiation

A piece of unleavened bread made from wheaten flour: that's what you have on the altar before the consecration — plain, ordinary bread. As soon as the priest — another Christ! — has said the words of consecration it is no longer a little piece of bread: it is Jesus Christ, true God and true man, with his body, blood, soul and divinity, as high and mighty as he is in heaven. Are our eyes deceiving us? No. What our eyes see, what our touch finds, what our senses show us is exactly the same as before — a certain shape, size, colour and taste. The *appearance* is the same as the *appearance* that little bit of bread had; but now, in spite of all appearances, that no longer is bread; it is not even a piece of bread which has been given symbolically a sacred presence and meaning. No, that *is* the body of Christ. It is not just that the bread is turned into body and the wine into blood but that they have been turned precisely into *the* body and *the* blood of Jesus Christ.

If God, on taking flesh, came down to our level, now, in shedding even his human shape to remain in the host, we can say that his self-abasement has brought him to put himself at a level lower than ours. As Ronald Knox points out (in *Pastoral Sermons*) he surrenders himself once again into men's hands, not by obeying with a human will but, if we might dare put it this way, by performing a kind of mechanical function we might expect of material things: he gives himself up not just as a servant but as an instrument, to be used by us and for us.

'By us and for us'. What had he said during the discourse at Capernaum? 'I am the living bread that comes down from heaven. Anyone who eats this bread will live for ever; and the bread that I shall give is my flesh, for the life of the world' (Jn 6:51). That's why our Lord gives himself to us as real, genuine food: so that we may have life. He puts it very clearly, to avoid any possibility of doubt, ambiguity: 'Anyone who eats my flesh and drinks my blood has eternal life, and I shall raise him up on the last day, for my flesh is food indeed, and my blood is drink indeed.'

I realise it is difficult to find words to express the immensity of the love which this marvel implies. It is so great a love that when you think deeply about it it makes you dizzy: it is so huge, so immeasurable by human standards. It would take a great theologian who was at the same time a great saint to find language able to get to the heart of it; it would call for all the piety and love which St Thomas Aquinas, for example, felt towards the Eucharist when he wrote the great hymn *Adoro te devote*. We need someone like that, especially nowadays in these confused years when, using the excuse of 'freedom of theological research', yet blatantly abusing that freedom, so many theories are being tossed around so frivolously and people so cleverly manage to avoid, in the name of some sort of ecumenism or philosophy, even the word 'transubstantiation.'

Food for the soul

Yes, we need some great saint to speak to us today about God's universal love for men, a limitless love which led him to divest himself of his human shape so he could stay with us in a tabernacle. A love which exposes him to indifference, loneliness, profanation and sacrilege, just so that we, so that each of us may be able to find him at any time, so that we can go to him when all else fails and we have nowhere to go, no one to help us, nothing to cling to. There we have him; he has become our food, to keep us alive. Who but a madman would think that he could live indefinitely without eating? Well, we also need food to keep a supernatural life going; this life is not tied to physical death but it can die through sin or lack of nourishment. He gives himself to us as food so that we may have life.

If we think about it another way and turn from God's attitude towards us (a love so great that it brings him to give himself to us as living bread) to the attitude we adopt towards him, the first thing we discover is an obvious contradiction between our faith and our behaviour. And the second thing is a sharp contrast between the generosity with which God treats us and the meanness, the stinginess with which we treat him.

Looking at our lives, at your lives and my life, at the lives of young people and older people around us, people we move among every day, the lives of the people who go busily about in cities and towns, looking at them dispassionately and with cold clarity, any non-believer might reach conclusions which may or may not be right but which are logical all the same. And they wouldn't be favourable conclusions.

Here we have, he might say, men who are sure that Jesus Christ, true God and true man, is in the Eucharist in just as real a way as he was during his life on earth among his apostles, among the crowds who listened to him, among those who benefited from his miracles. They are sure (because that is what the faith they profess tells them) that the greatest thing they can do in life is receive the Eucharist, because in it they receive God himself; they know that there is nothing in the world more important than this — no wealth, no success, no business can stand comparison with it. They know — as theology puts it for them — that one drop of divine grace far exceeds in value the whole universe with all the treasures it contains. And yet, it doesn't look as though they do believe this: not from the way they carry on; for, having so great a treasure within reach they don't even seem to bother to reach for it to make it their own. If you told them that in a particular place there was a huge amount of money there for the asking many would go after it through cold and wind, and rain and heat, not counting the difficulties, so hopeful they'd be of getting rich. Yet most people don't make the least effort to obtain something much more valuable.

Of course, anyone thinking along those lines would not be taking into account original sin, human weakness and many other things. Yet, in spite of all that, we'd still be inconsistent. In the penny catechism I used to read as a child one of the conditions given for making a good communion was to 'know and ponder on what you are going to receive.' Knowing, fine: but pondering . . .? Isn't it true that we rarely think about it, if we think about it at all? Most of us, surely, are like someone who has a great fortune and who is so busy, so distracted by little things, that he has completely forgotton about his wealth and is going around hungry and dirty and in tatters. Or it can also happen (very rarely I think) that our respect for this great Sacrament is such that we become conscious of our unworthiness and we refrain from receiving it. But if a child had such great respect for his parents and was so aware of how bold he had been (as is normal with children) that he never dared kiss them, I don't think that would make them very happy.

As far as most young people are concerned that is not what usually happens. If you took the trouble to look at yourselves and your friends, you'll find that the interest you show in receiving the living bread and having eternal life is considerably less than what you feel for a mere trifle. And yet our Lord said: 'I tell you most solemnly, if you do not eat the flesh of the Son of man and drink his blood, you will not have life in you' (Jn 6:53).

'You will not have life in you.' Naturally, he is talking about supernatural life, eternal life. And the obvious meaning of the words is that the reception of the sacrament is indispensable: he who receives this spiritual food has eternal life, he who does not receive it does not have eternal life. This is all very clear. There is absolutely no difficulty. Well then, why do so many Catholics stay away from the Eucharist? How can you explain why they have so much time for so many useless things; how they can waste their time so readily and not find a few minutes to speak to Jesus each day or to receive him? Perhaps the obvious answer, at least apparently, is this: they are not interested in him. It doesn't send me, it's a bore, it says nothing to me. I don't find it meaningful, etc., etc. To sum up, the having or not having of eternal life does not seem nowadays to be a subject which, among Catholic students, occupies even as important a place as spending time at student meetings. And as for other age groups: drinks, dining out, golf engagements, render them so busy that they too have no time.

How do you treat God?

You hear a lot of talk nowadays about the generosity of young people — although this is nothing new, for young people have always been said to be generous. But generalisations are dangerous. One — and I refer also to young people — can be very generous in some things and very mean in others. There are those who are very generous with their time and very mean with their money; and vice versa. It is true that greed, calculation and thrift are not usually characteristic features of youth. With all their life still ahead of them, with less attachments than older people, with their ideals still intact, with few responsibilities, young people tend to give themselves impetuously, even without thinking much about it. Perhaps that's what they mean when they say young people are generous. One thing is clear: young people are not conservatives. They cannot be and have no reason to be conservatives; for one thing they have not yet had the opportunity to do anything which is worth conserving.

But even granting that young people are generous I can't see that they are generous to God. Vis-à-vis God, generous giving is a rare commodity. How do young people in fact respond to God's love towards us which brings him to total self-abasement in the Eucharist (can you imagine any greater defenselessness, any greater surrender into man's hands?). There is an old saying that love is paid by love. If we know a tree by its fruit, my impression is that the love they have for the Eucharist is not very great: it's very small, in fact. Nor are things improving, at least not in my own country. One would have expected more from that adult Christianity which we hear so much about — a greater appreciation of such basic truths as this one, and more consistency in one's behaviour: but so far, at any rate, this adult Christianity has not yet produced any good results, at least not in this area (of eucharistic piety).

Sometimes I even ask myself if our attitude towards God become living bread to give us life is not too contemptuous. Don't misunderstand me. I am not referring to the contempt born of hatred, intentional or conscious contempt (it does exist and it is diabolical, the result of hatred of God). I refer, rather, to ignoring him, giving him no importance, trivialising him as if he meant nothing more than a 'thing' that is kept in churches with a lamp burning — something which has nothing to do with us or our lives.

True, our God is a hidden God: he is found only by those who consciously or unconsciously, yet truly, seek him. He is so veiled by the appearances of bread and wine that only faith and love ('we believe because we love,' was how Newman put it) can penetrate the veils which cover him, and so discover his presence. Those who don't have faith and love are like blind people: they have before them a world full of colour and shape and life but they can't see it. Maybe God has wanted things to be this way so that here too we can choose with full freedom of choice, without being conditioned in any way, between the bread of life and so many other things: maybe he wants us to have the opportunity to show what we prefer.

But if the Church is passing through very difficult times maybe one of the causes is simply that we have so little life within ourselves: maybe instead of theorising, the best thing we could do would be to increase that life by taking the nourishment which our Lord so generously offers us. And then surely we will show our appreciation to God by listening to what the Gospel tells us and living as he tells us. One way or another, we don't know more than God, not even when it comes to deciding what is best for us. It would indeed be sad if our pretentiousness led to our staying away from the living Bread and we were only a collection of corpses.

Being hated by the world

All of you, I suppose, have heard some time or another an expression which was very much in fashion during the years of Vatican Council II and is still popular with those Catholics who go in for criticising the Church. I refer to the word 'triumphalism' (and its derivatives). It is an expressive word, very good for throwing at an opponent: it turns the public immediately against him.

I do not wish to talk about this subject now (or ever, probably) but I certainly would want you to notice that, in one sense, and leaving aside the *ism,* every Christian cannot but have a certain interior feeling of assurance, of certainty that his faith will triumph. This should not stem from a vague feeling inside or from a crude fanaticism: we should have it because the Gospel teaches us that Jesus rose from the dead — this is no mere claim but a definite fact; because he said that 'Heaven and earth will pass away, but my words will not pass away'; because St Paul recalls that, 'if God is for us, who is against us'; because St John also wrote that the Lord, foreseeing events, said, 'In the world you will have affliction. But take courage, I have overcome the world.' I could give you many more reasons, but that would only be tiresome and would not add an iota to the value or the strength of those which I have quoted. One word from Christ is sufficient.

The Church has been faithful

No one who has studied the history of the Church would doubt that, up to the present, it has fulfilled its mission. It has kept intact the deposit of revelation and has transmitted and taught it with absolute fidelity, without taking away nor adding anything; it has constantly communicated to the people the divine life through the ministry of the sacraments and has been offering the sacrifice of the Son in reparation for the sins of the world; it has reigned with the love and solicitude of a mother over the portion of humanity entrusted to her, while still preaching the Word to all the nations, teaching them how to observe whatever Jesus has taught.

All this the Church has been doing for the past twenty centuries and has done despite all the odds, despite people's lack of understanding, despite the snares laid by people with power in this world to reduce her to an instrument of the state, despite persecution or martyrdom, despite also, the treachery, disloyalty, defection, weakness or coldness of some of her children, clergy included.

But the Church — the people of God, the mystical Body of Christ — who knows that her triumph is assured, also knows that this will always be at the price of sacrifice or, to put it better, at the price of the cross. I daresay this is something we, her children, have forgotten, particularly in this present time when those who try to de-mystify and desacralise the religion of Christ are also trying to reduce that religion to a modest humanism of a sociological or anthropological type which can be 'inserted' in the irreligious society around us, in the hope, no doubt, of converting it to Christ by easy stages.

So let me remind you of a very illuminating passage in the Gospel of St John, for it seems that we have all forgotten it. Our Lord said: 'If the world hates you, know that it has hated me before you. If you were of the world, the world would love what is its own. But because you are not of the world, but I have chosen you out of the world, therefore the world hates you. Remember that word that I have spoken to you: No servant is greater than his master. If they have persecuted me, they will persecute you also; if they have kept my word, they will keep yours also' (Jn 15:18-20).

It doesn't sound encouraging, does it? And yet, in one of the darkest moments in our Lord's life, in those hours which preceded his arrest, when he was bidding farewell to those close to him and was speaking to them from his heart, he showed this panorama to his disciples so they would know what to do; so there would be no misunderstanding. He does not promise them a triumphant career in the world; at least not in the sense in which the world understands success. It is precisely the opposite; it is in the life beyond that the triumph obtained by the disciples of the Gospel over the spirit of this world will be manifested.

Worldly success for the Gospel

There is one sense of the word 'triumph' which does not correspond exactly with what we usually imply when we use it in ordinary conversation. If we look closely, it is not difficult to perceive that in recent years (and also now in our own day) it seems as if people are indeed aiming at worldly success for the Gospel, using the word 'success' or 'triumph' in the sense the world uses it. So much has been said about the de-Christianized masses, of the 'failure' of the Church, the value of Marxism, the Church's need to adapt itself to the world if it is not to be left behind, at a standstill: so much has been said along these lines that there are Catholics, even ecclesiastics, who preach not the conversion of the world to God to become part of the Church, the city of God, but a conversion of the Church to the world. This would mean taking up the values of the world even at the expense of expurgating the Gospel.

This could be one way or *the* way towards a triumph of the Church *in* the world (but not *over* the world); and really, if there is any attitude that can properly be called triumphalistic, it is that of those who aspire to that state of earthly blessedness where the Church, adapting itself to all the criteria, to all the postulates, and to all the exigencies of the world, is fully integrated into that world. The only shadow that lies over this very nice prospect is that neither Jesus nor his Church nor the Gospel have anything to do with this kind of success.

The life of the Church in the world, if it can be expressed this way, is swimming against the current. That is the way it always has been. I am making nothing up when I assure you that the life of every Christian in the world has got to be like that of his Mother, the Church; swimming against the current, always and everywhere, provided he wants to live in accordance with his faith. Nobody has ever said that following the doctrine of Christ, keeping to the spirit and the teachings of the Gospel, is an easy thing. You all are aware that our Lord himself was careful to disabuse his disciples of any kind of enthusiastic idealism, any rosy triumphant notions, when he spoke to them. He was very clear: he told them what they could expect in exchange for their loyalty to him: hatred, persecution, failure.

Christ was a failure

Failure? That depends on how you look at it, I think. For if we measure things, events, with the standards of this world — and this is something a Christian cannot do unless he abandons the standards of the Gospel — then, certainly, our Lord's life was, quite clearly, a failure, perhaps the greatest failure, the loudest ever recorded in history. I wonder whether any of you has ever thought about that appalling verse of St Matthew which records one of the exclamations of our Lord on the cross: 'My God, my God, why hast thou forsaken me?' A very tragic end and hardly glorious: judged and condemned by the Roman tribunal, executed on the scaffold with two common criminals; betrayed by one of his disciples, denied by another, abandoned by the rest. Only his mother, one disciple, the youngest, and some women stayed with him in that horrible hour: that was all he had left when he was put to a final test by those who had condemned him — 'If he is the King of Israel, let him come down now from the cross, and we will believe him': nothing happened. And to round it off, a cry of loneliness and anguish: 'My God, my God, why hast thou forsaken me?'

And yet, what by the world's standards was a sign of a great failure, was in fact a final triumph, a decisive blow against sin, against the spirit of this world, against death. What was a scandal to the Jews, and stupidity, utter foolishness, to the Gentiles, was salvation to us (as St Paul said: for us, for those who believe that Jesus is the Son of God). It was not the end but the beginning: 'Was it not fitting that the Son of Man go through those difficulties before entering his glory?' Had the Lord not said, referring to himself, that if a grain of wheat is not buried and does not die it will not bear fruit?

The disciples were very well instructed. Of this, there is no doubt. Before setting out on the mission entrusted to them, they knew perfectly well what they would be exposed to, what the world would pay for their service, the price they would have to pay for their loyalty to Christ, their Lord, and for their fidelity to the doctrine given to them to be taught to all men and to save them. They knew it: but we have forgotten it, I am afraid.

Today, we, who say we are disciples of Christ, do not seem to be very interested in this aspect of the Gospel. I must admit furthermore, that we priests of the Church, one of whose obligations is precisely to teach these things, are not fulfilling this mandate of preaching the Gospel of Christ as it has always been

69

taught by the Church. On the contrary, the impression that some of us give is that we are afraid that you will go away if we make hard demands. We seem to want to make the doctrine of Jesus Christ 'attractive,' leaving away in the background anything we figure you will not like or emphasizing those things which we think you will like. At times, we use phrases from the Gospel in order to speak to you about purely temporal problems or questions which are in the air in the hope we can drag you somewhere, although I can't guess where. But it is not words, but the Word which you should know above all.

Being committed Christians

It is, then, when one knows the Gospel — the word of God — that one begins to make sense of this erratic world and to discover the truth of that verse in the Scripture which says that there is nothing new under the sun. It is also then that one begins to realize what it is to be a Christian and all it implies: it is also then when one learns the first lesson if he is capable of grasping it: that to be a Christian is to be *irrevocably* — mind you — *irrevocably* committed to Christ. And there is no room for any kind of neutrality here, it is not possible not to take sides. In regard to problems of a purely temporal character, it is quite in order to be neutral, because they deal with matters of opinion, not of dogma; but it is absolutely out of the question in anything that refers to Christ: 'He who is not with me is against me, and he who does not gather with me, scatters.' He spoke as clearly as that, so that there would be no doubt on what to do.

It is understandable if you offer some excuse. Perhaps we have not taught you the doctrine of Christ very well. I sincerely believe that we priests have a tremendous responsibility before God for a thousand mistaken compromises (in the past) and for another thousand mistaken concessions (in the present); but it is you who will be the guilty party if you think that you are free from responsibility because of this. The Bible is a very cheap book and within the reach of everyone, not only of those who are reasonably well-off: any beggar can get a copy. I fear that there are many who call themselves Christians, that is, disciples of Christ, who do not know this book at all. And while that may be an excuse for someone who can hardly read, it is definitely not so for a university man. Perhaps this explains why some people's idea of the Gospel is as poor as the Catholicism they profess; it is also not surprising that they should not feel the least enthusiasm for their faith, to the extent of letting it die a slow death of starvation. Yet the fact that this can be explained does not mean that it is thereby justified, because you could have done something (a lot, in fact) but you did not do it.

The Lord conquered the world. His disciples did too and, conscientiously following the doctrine they had received, they moulded the world according to their faith, willing to pay the price of suffering which their attachment to Jesus Christ demanded of them; they did not commit themselves to mere opinions or theories.

Kneeling down before the world

But we are not following the same path. It is the world that is moulding us to its image and likeness; we have given pride of place to success, money, standard of living, prestige, triumph, personal fame, comfort: these are the prime objectives worth fighting for (at least, so it seems judging by the interest, the time and the effort which we put into them).

These we take as *objectives,* whereas they are in fact nothing but consequences. Maritain was right when he spoke of that new type of contemporary Christianity (including a new type of ecclesiastic) which kneels down to the world, in ecstasy over its attainments, its progress, its technology. It is for this reason perhaps, that the world no longer hates us: our lives do not constitute a negation of its postulates and an affirmation of the Gospel.

But please observe that if the world despised our Lord, our Lord, in turn, did not despise the world. The world may hate us but we cannot pay back in the same coin, for we are children of God, and 'God loved the world so much he did not hesitate to give his only Son in order that we all may believe in him, may be saved and may live an eternal life. He did not send his Son to the world to condemn the world; but that through his mediation the world may be saved.' And if God loved the world, that world which he created and found good and loved to that extreme, how could we hate it? Jesus Christ died in order to save it from the chaos and the evil in which sin had submerged it, in order to make of it a place where men could live in peace as brothers, as children of one Father who live in the same house. I don't see how we can help to save it if we are so possessed by it that we are no longer capable of seeing in the Church of Christ anything except her structure, which we even condemn her for.

Those who understand (or at least, those who are reputed to know) say that nowadays young people protest precisely against that rotten society all around them; that the 'healthy rebelliousness of the youth' is aimed against social conventions, against the meaninglessness of the consumer society we live in, against certain unjust, hypocritical and selfish structures. I suppose that they do not include among that youth the thousands upon thousands of fans of pop stars, the multitude of young people whose increasing purchasing power is enriching the singers, musical groups and recording houses through the staggering sales of L.P.s and singles. I mention this, because this sector of youth seems to be one of the products of the consumer society which finds itself most at home with it and gives it all its support. But I cannot say to what extent we can include in this 'healthy rebelliousness', those poetic and somewhat erring young people who do not work, who use drugs, who abuse sex, who are given such a boost by the media. The youth of the working class doesn't seem to fit into it either. The truth is that young people of that type are so busy working, holding down their jobs, that they don't find time to solve the problems of the universe because they need all their resources for their own improvement. The youth that protests, it seems, is fundamentally college youth or pre-college youngsters.

Reforming the world's structures

Very well. Undoubtedly, there is a lot to be done. There is a lot to reform, a lot to improve. But how? I fear that the reform of structures is just a good excuse some people make (many, few? I wouldn't know) for not attending first to reforming themselves, making that change which the Gospel demands and which each of us should bring about within himself (helped by grace, because otherwise it is a useless effort). Yet that is the only way — self-denial. Take the cross and follow Christ in order to change, really and efficaciously, a world with all its structures, as our forefathers, the first Christians, did. They had faith enough in Christ to pay attention to him and to live according to his teaching, and this gave them the fortitude to pay the price.

It is true that it took them centuries, blood (theirs and not others'), untold humiliations (for them, not for others), misunderstandings and scorn; but they already knew that following Christ was not going to earn for them the affection of the world. They changed the world and succeeded in doing it without destroying, without condemning, without harming, without ire and without resentment, but yes, with faith in Christ, with much prayer, with infinite patience, devoting themselves to daily tasks well done, with privations, with a great capacity for understanding the mistakes of others, always forgiving and with love. To tell the truth, they never set out to change the structures. They simply changed men and the rest followed, as an inevitable and necessary consequence. The world — 'this world' — hated them, persecuted them, martyred them just like their Master; they, like their Master, loved it to the extent of bearing all things that it might be saved. And also, like the Master, they conquered the world.

As for us, if we seek success in the style of the world, the triumph of the Church *in* the world, a triumph of justice through changing structures, aside from heading for failure and working (in vain) to 'adapt' the Gospel, we would have wasted time and effort on something totally ephemeral. Structures are important, nobody doubts that. And if they are bad, defective, unjust and oppressive, they should be changed because they are the context in which people have to live and work: they exist not to stand in the way, but to help people. Let us not approach the problem superficially or be so naive as to believe that it is enough to change the source in order to purify the water. It is not the outward things that soil a man; the structures only reflect what man has inside him: his concept of God, of the world, of the things, of men, of their relationship, of existence itself.

Let us not fool ourselves. If a problem is well stated, there is every chance that it will be well solved; but if it is incorrectly posed, it takes a miracle to find an adequate solution. If we want to save the world, this world which we find so unjust, we must not sign a pact with it, because the first requirement is that we ourselves be saved; and we make a pact with it when we refuse to root out of our own selves our own injustice and selfishness, the law of least resistance, and pride, anger and sensuality; in short, all those criteria so accepted nowadays and so deeply rooted in us.

There is nothing you can do, I assure you, nothing worth doing, as long as you do not know the Gospel; as long as you do not make an effort to live in consonance with it; as long as the theories of the intellectuals have more influence on you than the Word of God. You will see for yourselves whether it is worth getting involved. One thing I'll say: if you do, you can be sure that the whole scene will change radically because you will have changed and, once that has happened, you will be able to initiate change around you. If you don't take the Gospel to heart, you can change all the structures, all the conditions, but everything will go on as before: worse than before. A million selfish men, greedy, unjust, lustful and violent, will continue to produce a violent, selfish, unjust, greedy and lustful society no matter how different the structures may be. It is not a matter of changing the dead, inert products of men; these must be changed but each person must start with himself. After all, ourself is what we have closest at hand and over which we all, absolutely all (not just minorities), have some power. The rest will come later, as an added extra, a necessary result.

What is truth?

A careful reading of the reports of the trial of Jesus is more instructive than we might think. Naturally, his sentence and execution attract more attention than the trial itself — but the trial is very well worth reading. Particularly the cross-examination of Jesus by Pontius Pilate, the answers he gave, the dialogue (or was it a case of pressurising?) between the Roman procurator and the Jews and, lastly, that final scene where a disgruntled and nervous judge washes his hands in a useless and miserable attempt to throw responsibility on others' shoulders: a whole series of very interesting lessons.

If we look at Pilate's behaviour overall, we find certain inconsistencies which must surely have an explanation. He was convinced of our Lord's innocence, yet he condemned him to death; he wanted to save Jesus but not at the expense of displeasing the Jews outside who were clamouring for his head; he showed him sympathy but not enough to take any risk on his behalf.

Pilate was not really an evil person but a man without quality, weak, self-suiting and probably a coward. The more one thinks about his attitude during the trial the clearer is the impression that as a man, he was not worth much. Of course, as far as he was concerned, he was quite ready to set our Lord free; if he did not do so it was out of fear of the harm he would do himself, the nuisance those Jews could cause. He seemed well-disposed towards Jesus: kindness, sympathy, a desire to set him free; the furthest things from Pilate's mind was to do Jesus any harm. Is this not exactly what we mean when we say: 'He is good at heart'? But Pilate's good feelings did not help at all except to add more humiliation, insult and beatings, which could possibly have been avoided if he had condemned him quickly and efficiently.

Let me draw your attention to a brief text by St John on this civil trial of Jesus. This may help us to understand Pilate's attitude better. It refers to the question Pilate addressed to Jesus, though I don't think it was really a question, in spite of its interrogative form, because it doesn't seem to expect an answer. Pilate asked Jesus: 'You are then a king?' Jesus answered: 'You say it; I am a king. This is why I was born, and why I have come into the world, to bear witness to the truth. Everyone who is of the truth hears my voice.' Then Pilate said to him: 'What is truth?' And no sooner did he say this than he again addressed the Jews (Jn 18:37 and 38).

Yes indeed, what is truth? With a gesture of elegant displeasure, Pilate left those few words in the air; they were not so much an honest question as a confession of his scepticism. Pilate did not believe in truth. On what ground, then, did he have to stage a battle to set an innocent man free? Not in the name of justice! There is no justice without some valid, true principles for all and for always, without some true facts. The Roman procurator was not a man whose attitude accorded with some principles, or ethics, much less any religious belief. And because he had no objective truth to cling to, no solid point of reference which he could hold on to securely, his attitude was fluctuating, self-accommodating, circumstantial, because he could move only within a meaningless field of relative factors which he had to sort out in the way that suited *him* best.

Jesus' words did not awaken in him the least attention, not even a speck of curiosity. Neither was he, apparently, an open man (except perhaps for superstition: the only thing that disquieted him seriously and inspired fear in him during the trial was the message from his wife telling him that she had a dream). However, had he taken the trouble to find out the meaning of the words uttered by our Lord, had he continued inquiring instead of throwing out questions to people who could not answer them, he would have found out that truth does exist. Indeed, he might have seen that he had before him the Truth himself: 'I am the way, and the truth, and the life,' Jesus had said. Jesus had come for that: to bear witness to the Truth, that is, to bear witness to himself: 'You bear witness to yourself,' the Jews told him. Our Lord's meaning totally escaped Pilate. Truth, at times, can seem very strange to minds not used to it or not open to it, so strange that it is not recognized even when it lies right before our eyes.

I ask myself if those words, which slipped over the thick slate of Pilate's scepticisim, have awakened in us a greater attention than they merited from him. In our days, the search for truth is not an objective for most people. Their scale of values contains things that they consider much more urgent and immediate, and much more important too: success, efficiency, money, popularity (which today we equate with publicity), pleasure, comfort, politics, power. Nor is it easy to find, nowadays, the restful patience that one needs for cultivating the mind, enriching it by investigating the bits of truth we find around us. People nowadays are practical, and they look for practical results. Technology, inventions and the sale of goods: these are really practical things. Besides, people are in a hurry: the longer it takes to obtain a positive result, the more it costs. How, then, would they devote themselves to the search for truth which requires so much effort, time and patience?: it is just not worth the investment.

Our time is characterised by what Peter Wust called 'the modern curse of subjectivism'. Luther did a disservice to truth when he introduced the principle of private interpretation, when he discarded the authority of the Church as the infallible interpreter of revelation and decided that every Christian who reads the Bible is aided by the Holy Spirit to interpret it correctly. From that moment on, that moment which initiated the Modern Age, people believe less and less in the truth; on the other hand, everyone believes more and more in *his* truth. Ever since Hegel put an end to even the most evident truths — like the principle of identity, the principle of non-contradiction — in order to erect in their stead *his* truths which were neither evident nor demonstrated, scepticism and relativism have not just spread: in some ways they have acquired the category of dogmas for those who reject the dogmas of revelation.

Nowadays man, especially the young person, finds himself with nothing solid to cling to. He cannot find firm rock under his feet to give him support, a basis to build his life on. All there is is sand, shifting sand, apparently useful today, really useless tomorrow and always deceiving and a source of despair. 'At any rate, it is *my* truth,' they say. Yes, and often it is a lie simply because it is a false truth: it is *his* but it is not true. For a long time now, one system for another, one theory after another has been built on clay. When an objectively real truth is not recognized which could serve as a test for hypotheses and systems, then there is no criterion and we feel lost in a world where everything fluctuates, where everything loses strength as soon as the winds change direction, where nothing is firmly rooted. In place of truth which is forever and for everyone, we get only impressions, feelings, opinions, theories, emotions, hypotheses and instability, everything fluctuating. Modern man's misery is a frightening misery, a sinister legacy he passes on to the youth of today.

What is truth? Pilate had it before his eyes and he was incapable of seeing it. It would be encouraging if young people felt a desire to find the truth again in the midst of the confused mess of inconsistent relativism. Much that is written about youth today seems to point at the fact that in the midst of their tremendous disorientation there is a sort of sixth sense which makes them react against falsehood and hypocrisy, a kind of desire for *authenticity* which expresses itself, if we can believe the diagnosis of many sociologists, in the repudiation (or should we say 'the rejection'?) of a conventional, hypocritical society as being devoid of true values. According to this diagnosis, hippies, long hair, bizarre dress, protest songs, the generation gap and even drugs, the blurring of sexual differences, and dirt would all be expressions of authenticity. Conventionalisms are rejected as being lies. Youth loves truth.

I wish to God that it were true! But I don't think it is quite as simple as that. To begin with, I fear that in many instances or, if you prefer, in many of these forms, spontaneity is confused with authenticity, genuineness. If someone is a liar and lies habitually because lies are what come out of him spontaneously, would we say that he is authentic? An authentic liar — that's what he is. If someone is lazy, cruel or vicious, is it a desirable quality (for authenticity is very desirable) to live without working, to abuse the weak or to indulge one's vices? To confuse authenticity with spontaneity is like saying that someone is sincere because he always says what he thinks, without ever thinking what he says. This is not being sincere but empty-headed.

Authenticity refers not to spontaneity but to truth. A pearl is authentic when it is a pearl, that is, when it is the excretion produced by an oyster; but when the pearl is produced artificially by man, then it is not genuine but false. Being true to one's self is, no doubt, one of the aspects of authenticity, though not the only one. But if you look closely this is more or less what is meant by the expression 'metaphysical truth.' Something is true when it is what it is; and something is authentic when it is what it should be.

There are other aspects. A colour-blind person sees red as green and sees it very clearly. He will continue seeing it that way no matter how well others explain his mistake to him and even if he notices that everyone else disagrees with him. Would you say he was being authentic if he stays in the ivory tower of his error, refusing to listen to everyone telling him he is wrong? I'd call it stubbornness, not authenticity. If that were authenticity, a fool should behave as a fool as much as possible, in order to be authentic and, if that's the case, I can't see how authenticity could be considered to have any value. I would say rather that the man who has courage to recognize that he may be wrong, the man who is capable of admitting that his ideas may be wrong in spite of the clarity with which he sees them, the man who has the courage to correct his mistake and does not worry what people think of him: he is authentic. In other words, a person behaves authentically when he adheres to reality, whether he likes it or not; and he behaves in an unauthentic manner when he fools himself, consciously or unconsciously, with ideas, dreams or theories which, because they do not conform to reality, constitute an artificial world. One can be absolutely convinced that two and two make seven and act consistently with his conviction, but this does not make him authentic. The mind's adjustment to the reality of things is, then, another ingredient or another aspect of authenticity. And this is precisely what is meant by the expression 'logical truth.'

Sincerity

Finally, we could talk about sincerity as another facet of authenticity. A hypocrite who pretends to be what he is not, who assumes an attitude, who deceives others, is a two-faced man. He is two-faced even if his hypocrisy, pretense and deception are servants of an ideology and merely used as means to achieve some higher purpose. A person who lies is a liar; he is false. He is false, because what he says does not express what he thinks and feels: it doesn't matter what motives lie behind his behaviour, whether it be for the triumph of an ideology or of a political party or of a commercial product. This type of truth, the fitting in of what he says to what he thinks, this moral truth is another aspect of authenticity and of course it is not much practised nowadays.

Truth, authenticity. What is the relation between the two?

The youth of today, men and women, do they seek truth? Or, do they simply put the accent on authenticity, understanding it simply as the sincere expression of what they feel or think at any particular time? If that were so, then all rudeness, any gesture of bad manners, even the crudest expression of selfishness can be praiseworthy because it carries the stamp of authenticity. So if young people put at the top of their scale of values *authenticity* taken in that sense, then it would be well for us not to trust them very far because you don't need to go very far along that route to reach the fanaticism of the Hitler Youth or the Maoists: for then it is not truth which matters but the expression of what one believes and feels, even if that means lying and cruelty.

No. Authenticity has to do with truth. Pieper puts it very well: 'Truth', he says, 'is nothing other than the expression of being.' And I would say that authenticity is the expression of truth. Therefore, if you express something which is false, there is no authenticity involved.

Of course, truth is no longer fashionable nowadays, probably because we have created so many needs for ourselves that there is no more time to search for it. Besides, truth can be very uncomfortable and, for a society where comfort is almost the supreme value, any discomfort must be rejected because it makes no sense. But look how easily Pilate got out of it! What is truth? It must be something that involves commitment: whereas scepticism, relativism, means that you never have to commit yourself to anything. Everything is fluid; you can move freely from one position to another, from one principle to another; you can use any principle, any standard, that suits you in any situation, and then shed it when the situation changes. But man remains and, in the long run, he ends up empty and tired of so much fleeting change and useless effort. He has to be constantly elaborating theories to substitute those that have ceased to work and, in the end, it all turns out to be an empty game in which one moves from one bankruptcy to another.

To speak about truth and about being must undoubtedly smell of Thomistic-Aristotelian philosophy and I fear that this is not the best introduction to encourage you to like it — after all, you belong to this world of today. However, you could fall into worse philosophies; this philosophy of being, because it is realistic, has at least the advantage of being on the side of common sense. And when common sense is missing, talking becomes unintelligible.

Truth must be captured, seized by each person individually. At times its erruption is disconcerting, painful or irritating because truth obliges. It demands an effort. Access to truth requires many renunciations from man (above all, it means saying 'no' to superficiality, laziness, comfort, over-indulgence . . . and sin). Consequently, he needs to keep up an interior struggle because in man and in his surroundings there are forces that tend to obstruct his openness to the truth, forces which make him close the eyes of his soul to the clarity of what is, of Who is: for every truth has, in some way, a divine dimension, because everything which exists, exists by virtue of God, and it is true to the extent that it conforms with the divine mind. Authenticity means, in the final analysis, living according to the truth; thus when one acts according to the truth, one eventually accedes to the Truth: 'he who does the truth comes to the light.' Isn't it very significant that Jesus should merge into one condemnation (because of their inter-dependence) pharisaism, falsehood and the devil? He said: 'The father from whom you are is the devil . . .there is no truth in him . . . he is a liar and the father of lies.' Nor is there any truth in the Pharisees, that is, in hypocrites, all those who keep up a front which belies what is behind it.

Whether you know it or not, everyone who honestly seeks the truth is seeking Christ and, and if only he searches honestly and courageously, he will find himself. He follows the narrow path because, in order to reach the truth, he has to renounce all the easy-going ways involved in accepting any ideology that exempts him from thinking too much and that allows him, on the other hand, to justify certain weaknesses. By searching for the truth, moreover, a person is no longer a robot, someone who stops using his head and allows himself to be manipulated like a depersonalized fragment of a mass. He does not subject himself to a self-appointed orator, to a leader who shouts slogans or to some genius who whispers in his ear that he should ask for or what he should do.

That is why the act of thinking with your own intellect, of investigating, of inquiring into the truth, is very important nowadays, and especially important for you. If at your age you already act like a mere mass with a mob mentality, you are lost. You'll never escape that mortal trap that tends to obliterate the most noble and great that there is in man — his intellect and his will.

In this era where, due to mass technology and mass psychology, man is treated as a thing (wasn't it Hitler who said that one lie, repeated a thousand times, is accepted as truth?), the search for truth is the best pursuit for anyone who wishes to be a man and not an object, because it is a task so absolutely personal that the mere act of doing it prevents us from being reduced to a mass. It is love for the truth, fidelity to the truth, that prevents one from being caught up in the chaos of the environment. It is this that provides firm ground, ground for hope for those who do not wish to perish in the sea of subjectivism; a spot that can be held on to by those who already are tired of rolling over the incessant flow of meaningless situations. I don't think that any college student wants to become like Pontius Pilate (unless I am absolutely wrong about the youth of today).

The truth shall make you free

If you ever get to read the eighth chapter of the Gospel of St John, you will have a great time, at least from the intellectual point of view. I don't mean, of course, the kind of reading that is careless and hurried, but one that is leisurely, attentive and with enough time for reflection whenever the occasion requires it — which will be often. And of course, an unprejudiced reading, done with an open and a receptive mind.

This is the chapter which reports a remark Jesus made in passing: nevertheless, it angered the Pharisees, who were rather inclined to anger. This is what it says: 'Jesus therefore said to the Jews who had come to believe in him, "If you abide in my word, you shall be my disciples indeed, and you shall know the truth, and the truth shall make you free"' (Jn 8:31-32).

This last statement was what provoked his listeners to anger, leading to a discussion between Jesus and the Pharisees. The profound meaning of this statement — 'the truth shall make you free' — was explained by Jesus himself in the course of the discussion. What Jesus is saying can be deduced from the context itself to mean this: God created man free; man was induced to error (he thought he could become equal to God) by the devil, 'a liar and the father of lies,' committed sin and at that very moment lost his freedom, because 'everyone who commits sin is a slave to sin'. But a slave cannot free himself; he has to be freed by someone with sufficient power to do so. That someone is the Son — who is the way, *the truth,* and the life: only he can redeem man from sin and, through grace, bring him back to the state of liberty, breaking the bonds of sin which imprisoned him: 'If therefore the Son makes you free, you will be free indeed.'

What does 'freedom' mean?

If we are to judge by the number of times the word 'freedom' is used nowadays, we can say that freedom is a subject very much in vogue. And what our Lord says about it is very thought-provoking. 'The truth shall make you free.' And falsehood? Can a lie make someone free? Can a person whose ideas of freedom are based on a falsehood and therefore on a false notion of freedom consider himself *truly* free?

If we are to believe what we read nowadays, young people (or at least, some of them) don't feel free; they feel imprisoned and frustrated by certain structures which they did not themselves create, a system in which they had no say. But I don't think this only happens with young people; some of us older people (or if you prefer, some adults) don't find it pleasant either to be in ugly and large cities, built of cement and asphalt, planned, it would seem, for traffic which spews out smoke and noise; in a civilization where technology is flattening man down and subjecting him to its goals. We also see ourselves choked by rules, ordinances and bureaucratic red tape. It is very understandable why some young people return to a kind of nomadic lifestyle: they leave that world made up of rules, pertrified conventions and unnecessary needs which are forever increasing in number. But even if they *feel* more free, are they really? Does being free consist simply in the cutting off of all ties, all links with everything?

What does being free really mean? A man without a family to support; without a country in which to sink his roots; without a faith to keep to; without a moral norm to sustain him; without an objective truth to which to relate; without a love to give himself to; without hope with which to fight; without a God whom to love: a man like that, so free from everything, would he really be a free man?

No. He would not be. He would not even be a real man. He would be a kind of thing without any humanity in him and, of course, if anyone did live in such conditions, his life would be a real hell, an emptiness so horrifying that only a state of unconsciousness would make it even bearable. A man like that would be a kind of thing without any humanity in him and, hold on to the most basic things, just to have some contact with reality but at the same time avoiding at all costs anything that would make him aware that his life was empty; that it had no direction; that it made no sense.

Freedom is not defined by the absence of all bonds, of all

ties. It is not simply a word. Freedom is a reality existing in a world of realities; of other realities which one cannot ignore nor be independent of because these also exist and they also matter. The freedom of man has an origin; it has an object to which to apply itself; it has a purpose that gives it sense. To ignore such basic realities is equivalent to denying or destroying freedom. To be free does not mean to be all-powerful and to do whatever one wants. Even if he wants to, no one can do whatever he feels like doing, but that does not stop him from being a free man. Man is a limited being, so how can his liberty be unlimited? That is why every limitation, any limitation, need not be an insult to freedom.

Freedom is not independence

Besides, freedom is not strictly the same as independence. Man is free but he is not independent. He needs many things from other people in order to live, even in order to survive. He is a real being made in a specific way and he cannot change his nature unless he stops being a man. And besides there are other men who are also free and who have the right to have their freedom respected. Living with others always implies giving something up. The trouble with the word 'freedom' is that it is an ambiguous word, at least in a certain sense. Unless there is agreement as to the content and range of this concept, then all conversation becomes a dialogue between deaf men and, I am afraid, everyone has his own ideas of what freedom is. But what is authentic freedom, really?

If being free does not mean being all-powerful nor independent (in the most radical sense), then it is compatible with limitation and dependence. Actually, limitation and dependence are inborn in man by the mere fact of being man. Here we must quote some words of Gustave Thibon which give a true idea of what freedom is: 'We cannot be selfish; for that way we become prisoners. The miser we can see being devoured by gold; the libertine by woman; the saint by God. The problem is not whether to give ourselves or not; it is a question only of knowing who or what we are giving ourselves to.' Now, then: if every man is bound to something or to someone, the quality of his freedom will depend on the quality of the bond which ties him and which he freely chooses to be tied by. And this is so because freedom is exercised in the choice of two or more possibilities, one of which the will must choose, because it cannot remain indefinitely undecided. But it is not the will or freedom which chooses between two or more possibilities: it is reason. Reason is so basic to the use of freedom that there can be no freedom in the true sense except in rational beings. We cannot say that something irrational is free, whether a plant or a stone; even if a dog can go from one place to another; even if a plant grows freely. Free choice presupposes deliberation, reflection, consideration, evaluation of choices to be made. When this is not done, when the mind does not work, then there is no freedom: it is a matter, then, of appetite, caprice, instinct, whim, impulse, something which is not rational nor reasonable, something that is not entirely human.

And something like this is what happens nowadays. Saint Exupery has expressed it very well in *The Citadel:* 'Because to me it has been revealed that man is in every way similar to a citadel. He destroys the walls to ensure his freedom, but now he has become a dismantled fortress open to the stars. Then the anguish of not being free begins.' Open to the stars, but also open to all wind, without any shelter; and also open to the attack of enemies, without any defence. Today man, particularly some young people, has destroyed the walls that were protecting him and which were a guarantee of his integrity against all destructive forces. He has destroyed all the 'myths,' he has done away with 'taboos.' But in reality what he has destroyed, what he has annihilated in the name of freedom, is truth. And in order to be 'free,' he has replaced freedom by illusions, by dreams, by optimistic visions of the future, by theories as brilliant as they are empty of foundation. And the result?

Degradation

Well, it seems that never before has man felt less free than now. He has severed all ties which united and bound him to God. In so doing, he has enslaved himself to hideous degradation, to extremes such as justifying the use of drugs as a way to freedom; sexual perversion as a break from limitation; and the transgression of the natural laws as a victory of man. He opposes authority to freedom as if these were two incompatible enemies. He detests order and discipline as if order, discipline and obedience could not be the result of a freedom which is well-lived; as if these could not be freely, conscientiously and deliberately lived. A diabolical lie — 'the devil is a liar and the father of lies; there is no truth in him' — penetrates minds and darkens them. It is like a thick cloud which hides the truth and distorts it, which cripples and supplants it.

At the basis of this characteristic feature of our time, there is an unhealthy pride. It is the type of pride which has led people to diagnose the death of God and the maturity of humanity. Humanity has attained maturity and no longer needs a Father. But this is not progress, it is retrogression:

For the wrath of God is revealed from heaven against all ungodliness and wickedness of those men who in wickedness hold back the truth of God, seeing that what may be known about God is manifest to them. For God has manifested it to them. For since the creation of the world his invisible attributes are clearly seen — his everlasting power also and divinity — being understood through the things that are made. And so they are without excuse, seeing that, although they knew God, they did not glorify him as God or give thanks, but became vain in their reasonings, and their senseless minds have been darkened. For while professing to be wise, they have become fools, and they have changed the glory of the incorruptible God for an image made like to corruptible man and to birds and four-footed beasts and creeping things.

Therefore God has given them up in the lustful desires of their heart to uncleanness, so that they dishonour their own bodies among themselves — they who exchanged the truth of God for a lie, and worshipped and served the creature rather than the Creator who is blessed forever, amen.

For this cause God has given them up to shameful lusts: for their women have exchanged the natural use for that which is against nature, and in like manner the men also, having abandoned the natural use of the woman, have burned in their lusts one towards another, men with men doing shameless things and receiving in themselves the fitting recompense of their perversity. And as they have resolved against possessing the knowledge of God, God has given them up to a reprobate sense, so that they do what is not fitting, being filled with all iniquity, malice, immorality, avarice, wickedness; being full of envy, murder, contention, deceit, malignancy; being whisperers, detractors, hateful to God, irreverent, proud, haughty, plotters of evil; disobedient to parents, foolish, dissolute, without affection, without fidelity, without mercy. Although they have known the ordinance of God, they have not understood that those who practise such things are deserving of death. And not only do they do these things, but they applaud others doing them (Rom 1:18-32).

Well, perhaps today it is not correct to speak of man as a worshipper of four-footed beasts, birds and serpents; but of computers and of his other achievements; of his own theories on life and death and what there is after death. But otherwise the picture is no different from the times of St Paul. It is not a sign of hope but a dangerous symptom that the formulation of human rights should be considered as a great advancement (formulated in fact at the end of a war which gave so much evidence of inhumanity); it shows that these rights have been forgotten or left unexercised. And they still are, it seems to me.

If you read the newspapers, the whole world seems to be bent on becoming a real jungle. And modern man, so mature and so absolutely free, has taken the road toward a degradation never before known through the centuries. It is even worse because before Christ, who is the Truth, truth had not yet come. But now, he is despised as God even when he is sentimentally (or deliberately) admired as a man, as a good man.

Truth does exist.

But man's mind even if it can progress, cannot change reality. And reality is that Jesus Christ is the Son of God, true God, the absolute Truth. 'Let us consider what our freedom would be like if there really existed a truth, one sole truth, which would measure all other truths and without which these would cease to be truths.' (Singrid Undset). The truth does exist and it is a living Truth, but contemporary man rejects it. This Truth is the cornerstone and the stumbling block, but it is the only one that can give man freedom because it frees him from his own egoism. For a man is not really free when he does what he wants, but when he wants what he ought; since freedom refers not to the doing but to the wanting. The will must be completely free of attachments in order to apply itself to duty, which sometimes may not suit its taste, or its whims, or its comfort or its self-interest. It is this quality of freedom which gives the measure of the fulness of man, because a man who is truly a man does what he has to do, whether he feels like it or not and besides he is responsible for his acts, for there is no freedom where responsibility does not exist. Neither a child nor a deranged person can enjoy freedom because neither has the capacity to use his reason and that is why they are not responsible. It is symptomatic that nowadays when, in the name of freedom, all truth that is not scientific truth is rejected (small truths which essentially do not effect the being of man, even if these can destroy or heal him), the techniques to exempt him from responsibility for his acts have reached an unsuspected perfection.

Genuine freedom enjoyed only by saints

In the deepest recesses of his being, a man is always able to say yes or no, I want or I do not want, I accept or I rebel, and he can do this even if he is under severe external pressure. He can do it by virtue of the free will which each man has, by virtue of his being a rational creature made in the image and likeness of God. But *freedom*, true freedom, is enjoyed only by those who are free of all servitude to sin. Personally, I believe much more in the freedom of a saint (I think, for example, of St Teresa of Avila or St Francis of Assisi) capable of knowing the will of God — the truth — of wanting to do it and doing it in spite of everything, than in that of any fellow who calls himself free because he is not governed by anything except his blind impulses, his incoherent whims or his savage instincts.

When a man has no ties other than his attachment to God — the Supreme Truth — this man is the freest of all, because he shares in the truth of God and 'truth is not enchained.' This is the case with the saints. But there are no chains heavier than those of a man who is inexorably alone and without any roots, for 'freedom becomes arbitariness or caprice when truth is rejected; then egoism is converted into a norm.' To believe that one is free because he breaks the commandments of God, or he hits his neighbour when he feels like doing it, or because he vandalises the wall of someone else's house (never his own) in order to express his protest: this is proof only of impotence and of falsehood; that is, of slavery. Or could it be that the sensualist or the drug-addict or the violent person is free just because he breaks some rules? From what has he freed himself, we might ask?

'Freedom' is a big word, a word which enjoys a much greater prestige than the word 'truth.' This is why our time, which rejects truth in the name of freedom, does not know what it is to be authentically free. Never has sin been committed with more insolence (always, it is clear, in the name of freedom), but never — unless, perhaps, in the epoch described by St Paul in his epistle to the Romans — have men felt less free. Truly, the yoke that God imposes is infinitely sweeter and lighter than what we men impose on ourselves in the name of freedom.

In the last analysis, reality is what truly counts. If someone ignores it, he ends up injuring himself after fruitless argument. Voluntary acceptance of what one is, the humility of submitting oneself to the will of God, of accepting the truth with all its consequences, is the only road by which a person can find himself in freedom. In other words: rejection of Christ, whatever form it takes, is the best way to become a slave to a cruel master, call it ideology, passion, impulse or whatever.

If I dared give you some advice, I would tell those of you who have believed in Him to continue believing in Him, to persevere in his doctrine; then you shall *know* the truth and the truth shall make you free. And if there is anyone who wants to change this world — something which you seem very keen on — it will be people able to believe in the truth and, through it, to be truly free.

Crucify him!

In his account of the Passion St Luke explicitly names 'the chief priests and the rulers and the people' as those involved in the exchanges with Pilate, when Pilate tried to convince them of Jesus' innocence (not that he tried very hard). Pilate clearly knew that Jesus was not guilty of anything deserving death; for one thing the Jews' charge was very vague, and besides — unless he was an absolute fool — he must have been aware of Jesus' reputation, preaching and performing miracles, and well aware also of the Pharisees' enmity towards him.

It is curious, this conversation between Pilate and the Jews (if you can call it that when one side refuses to listen to any kind of reason). As soon as they pronounced judgement on Jesus they brought him before the governor; and Pilate, in his turn, examined Jesus, found no crime, and advised them accordingly. But the Jews kept at it, and when Pilate learned that he was a Galilean, he decided to dispose of the problem by sending him to Herod who had jurisdiction over Galilee. Herod examined him in turn, treated him with scorn — and sent him back to Pilate.

Up to this, you might say, was stage one in the trial. Pilate decided that Jesus was innocent and "he called together the chief priests and the rulers and the people and said to them, 'You brought me this man as one who was stirring up the people. Now I have gone into the matter in your presence and I can find no case against the man on any of the charges you bring against him. Neither did Herod, for he sent him back to us. As you can see, the man has done nothing that deserves death. Therefore I will release him.' "

Doesn't that seem to be a clear acquittal? On the one hand, it clearly does, because Jesus is declared innocent and Pilate's decision follows from that. And yet we are left with the impression that the matter is not settled: it almost looks as though Pilate were leaving the case open, pending confirmation by the people; it looks as though he's offering his opinion, waiting to see how the crowd reacts. He has not really pronounced a final verdict: he lacks the firmness of character it requires.

But he did want to save Jesus, 'for he knew it was out of envy that they had delivered him up' (Mt 27:18). Yet he also wanted to keep on the right side of the Jews: they were so fanatical that they could cause trouble and put his career in jeopardy. So he hit on a solution connected with the custom of setting free a condemned person in honour of the feast of the Passover. It was all a matter of setting some undesirable type alongside Jesus — someone the people could find just nothing good in — and, offered such a choice, how could they possibly opt for a man with the background and characteristics of Barabbas?

Perhaps Pilate was relying on the good sense of the crowd. He couldn't believe they would actually choose a plotter and a murderer instead of Jesus. If so, he hadn't taken account of the political skill of the chief priests and the elders who 'persuaded the crowd to demand the release of Barabbas and the execution of Jesus' (Mt 27:20).

The fact is that when he offered them the choice 'they all cried out, "Away with this man, and release to us Barabbas . . ." Pilate addressed them once more, desiring to release Jesus, but they shouted out, "Crucify him, crucify him!" A third time he said to them, "Why, what evil has he done? I have found in him no crime deserving death; I will therefore chastise him and release him." But they persisted, demanding with loud cries that he should be crucified. And their voices prevailed. So Pilate gave sentence that their demand should be granted. He released the man who had been thrown into prison for insurrection and murder, and whom they asked for; but Jesus he delivered up to their will' (Lk 23:18-25).

Losing oneself in the crowd

Leaving aside the question of the activity of the devil and the deeper causes of the crucifixion, I would like now for us to think a little about this aspect which Luke brings up. My own view is that the crowd, all worked up, shouting for Jesus' death, did influence Pilate's attitude. A handful of priests and a few elders could not, on their own, have exerted enough pressure to scare the governor: look what happened, some years later, in a similar sort of situation, in the case of St Paul. And, yet, did those people who were shouting like madmen 'Crucify him, crucify him!' really want Jesus to die? If Pilate had taken them aside and asked them one by one, do you think they would have chosen to set Barabbas free and kill Jesus?

I don't think so. A man does not behave the same way when he has to face up to a situation in a personal way as he does when he acts anonymously as an insignificant member of a crowd. In the first case he is acting as a person, using his intelligence and deciding with his free will (if he is courageous enough to do so) — and running the risk of having to answer for his personal acts (that's why courage is called for). In the second case, on the other hand, a man gets so depersonalised in a crowd that he does not act *like a human being*, i.e. intelligently and freely, and moreover does not run the risk of having to answer for what he does. This is a particularly good way to throw stones and hide your hand behind your back, an excellent way to dilute your responsibility even though you can do that only in the sight of men (you cannot avoid responsibility before God or before your conscience: of course, as far as your conscience is concerned you would have to be sufficiently sincere to face up to it).

On other occasions, when the people became all enthusiastic about our Lord's words or about his miracles, they even wanted to make him their king; now, however, they shouted, almost in hate, 'Crucify him!' On what grounds could they condemn him so brutally? Had they even listened to what Jesus had to say in his defence? Of course not.

These events look place on Good Friday, fairly early on. It is quite possible that many of the people who were there (Jerusalem was packed with pilgrims who had come from all over to celebrate the Passover) did not even know an hour beforehand that Jesus had been handed over to Pilate, and it is also possible that some of those who pressed around the praetorium, were, at least at the start, just curious, and, taken one by one, good people.

If they had been asked, individually, directly and without being got at, to decide on Jesus' fate, just on the basis of certain objectively established facts, would they have condemned him to a humiliating public execution, and also have set Barabbas free? They couldn't have. And yet these men, who on their own would not have hurt a fly, once they were in a crowd, started to act like animals: these rational men who were well able to distinguish good from evil and right from wrong, acted like fanatics, closed to all reason; these free men, who in their ordinary lives were quite capable of accepting responsibility for their actions, acted in a crowd like a flock of sheep which follows the mere whistle of whoever leads them. In that whole crowd there were only a few — the leading priests, the rulers, some Pharisees — who knew what they were doing and why they were doing it; but these were not part of the crowd: they were stirring up the crowd. They 'persuaded the crowd to demand the release of Barabbas and the execution of Jesus' (Mt 27:20).

And there was Pilate, the miserable creature, convinced that Jesus was innocent, yet scared by the shouting crowd; a miserable wretch who had the authority but lacked the character necessary for exercising it; who had the power to ensure his au · thority and was respected but he lacked the integrity needed to face unpopularity. A cowardly, vacillating man, afraid and weak who tried to avoid the issue by washing his hands like a sulking child who leaves the game because he can't keep on, because he only wants to win.

My feeling is that there has always been a lot of this sort of thing — nowadays also; I mean, people like Pilate, basically good people (he wanted to set Jesus free) but whose weakness does more harm to the innocent than does the malice of others. And people like that small group of Jews, the leaders of the crowd, in fact, who use the good faith, ignorance, superficiality or naivety of the crowd to further their own ends, their own mean ambitions; people who use the crowd as a shield, hiding behind it, acting anonymously and escaping from responsibility.

'Honourable men'

And then there is the crowd, the mass — like a blind animal, a many-headed monster, easily manipulated — something quite frightening in the way it rushes blindly after the victims whom its leaders single out. It's not that the crowd is made up of evil men: that is rarely the case. Someone once said that no revolution could ever happen without the cooperation of honourable men. In fact it is the presence of honourable men in an upheaval that sets families at ease, that reassures simple people who are peaceably engaged in their work and in helping bring up their families — people who have no time to be concerned about the big issues because urgent everyday affairs take up all their attention right through their lives. Yes, for any revolution you need honourable people, that kind of upright person, in no way malicious, usually idealistic; the sort of person who is a bit simple because he lacks critical judgement; he is unable to see further than appearances but he can be inflamed if the right words are used on him. Sometimes, also, a person who has a certain standing, who is less intelligent than he thinks he is, who may sometimes attract attention but for superficial reasons, not because of his real worth. You must have come across him sometime or other: a good person, personally incapable of violence of any type, who is as convinced that he is called to perform some important mission as he is incapable of realising that he is only fulfilling the role which other people allow him to take. This is just the type of stop-gap person who fades into nothingness as soon as his usefulness ceases. Time blots him out; if anyone does remember him it is with sorrow or perhaps irritation — never with admiration or appreciation, and sometimes not even with respect.

All these ingredients were there on this occasion: weak and insecure authority; people who were quite clear in their minds about what they wanted and who subtly stirred up the blind crowd and got them to support their plan; a crowd who did not know, who weren't thinking, but who shouted the slogans dished out to them, frightening the poor man whom Rome had sent them as governor, bending his weak will to their own. And also an innocent victim, ground out by the cowardice of one man, the hatred of a few and the stupidity of the crowd.

'Coming to oneself'

When it was all over things were seen in a different light. Not much is known about Pilate's reaction; the leaders of the people became even harder than they had been. As for the rest of the crowd, St Luke gives us a very interesting piece of information: 'And when all the people who had gathered for the spectacle saw what had happened they went home beating their breasts' (23:48). They beat their breasts. They realised they were guilty and they wanted to express their repentance. You don't beat your breast over something which has happened which you are not responsible for — over some unfortunate event in which you had no part. On the contrary, you beat your breast when you realise that you have done something harmful, for which you are guilty.

I don't know why these words of St Luke also remind me of another expression which the same evangelist uses at one stage in the parable of the prodigal son. When he had spent all his money he began to feel the pinch and he had to take up a job herding pigs; and then 'he came to himself,' he realised how crazy he had been. The Jews also who had flocked to Calvary to watch the 'show' of the crucifixion, when all was over, they too 'came to themselves.' An amorphous mass cannot stay indefinitely in an excited emotional state; and anyway a mass of that type is unstable. Sooner or later, the event which causes the crowd to form and keeps it together just dissolves like a lump of sugar.

It was then, after the excitement was over and all that was left was the evil done, that they realised that they had crucified an innocent man. They had called for, they had even demanded, Jesus' crucifixion. They had refused to listen to any kind of reasoning or real argument: they had drowned Pilate's words by their irrational roar. A crowd does not reason or reflect or think: a crowd only shouts. Is a crowd responsible for anything?

A crowd is not really a group of people who know what they want and where they are going; a crowd is not organised to achieve some goal it sets for itself, nor does it consciously obey the directives of its leaders. The 'people' who were there at the entrance to the praetorium were just a casual amorphous group of persons. And a person can indeed think and reflect, know and desire; a person is indeed responsible. It was not the crowd who beat their breasts going away from Calvary: it was 'all the people who had gathered for the spectacle.' The crowd had dispersed; it no longer existed; but the people remained: all those men and women who now realised that they had helped bring about the death of an innocent man on the gallows. It is obvious that when a man ceases to be a person, when he becomes depersonalised by becoming part of a crowd, he lets himself be led by emotions, by passion, and he does not realise much what he is doing or where his actions may lead. That is quite true. But, to what extent can you excuse his decision to become part of the crowd, knowing that he is abdicating his role as a person? Was it not his voice, were those not his shouts which pressurised that weak governor, making him betray his conscience and commit an injustice?

Cooperation in evil

I think there is a type of sin which all of us often commit and which we rarely confess, perhaps because, it is subtle and is very common and gets buried in the general atmosphere, our conscience (especially nowadays when all this mental chaos is not conducive to spiritual sensitivity) hardly gets a look in. And in addition to this, the practice of examination of conscience is not gone into for very much.

I refer to the sin of 'cooperation in evil.' One person's shout is nothing but without that shout and another and another no clamour ever develops. A shout can frighten a small child but you need a lot of people to work together to produce a roar, which can frighten a full grown adult and force him to do things he does not want to do or which he ought not to do. You cannot create an atmosphere with just one person, because an atmosphere is the result of the behaviour of many people, and all of us, in one way or another, contribute to its features.

A multitude of Jews created the atmosphere which made it possible for our Lord to be crucified: they all cooperated effectively and positively in perpetrating that terrible injustice. It rather looks as though today we generally recognise this phenomenon of massification, or depersonalisation of the individual, of the person: studies just keep pouring out on this subject: it is now an accepted fact. Perhaps it is this massification which explains how a few people can achieve such enormous influence on their environment, imposing on it their tastes, their interests, their ideas, their opinions, even their notions of right and wrong. They attain this power mainly due to passivity on the part of the mass who cooperate with them without thinking, without reacting. I have so often heard people comment on the theatre or on films saying, for example, 'How can the government allow these things to be put on?', but it is the people who, by paying money and going in, by their active cooperation, keep such shows on the road: it is they who are responsible for their success: and one success leads to another. We complain about the sharp decline in public morality: but is it perchance idolatrous pagans who are responsible for this corruption, or baptised sons and daughters of the Church? Who is it who helps promote the climate of confusion by spreading theories which are contrary to the basic teachings of the Church on faith and morals, even where the Vicar of Christ has spoken unequivocally — as in the case of contraceptives or celibacy of the clergy? Is it the pagans? Is it not the Christians, the Catholics, in the western world?

Small, well-knit, organised groups, who know exactly what they want and how to get there. An ever greater number of men and women who gradually are becoming part of a mass like Ionesco's rhinoceroses and who cooperate effectively in the attainment of the objectives of those small groups: they act as amplifiers of their shouting — through their ignorance, their remarks, their snobbery, their empty-headedness, their coward-ice (they don't dare swim against the current), their love of comfort. And also authorities who are weak or vacillating or lacking in standards, who keep quiet, who don't want to be inconvenienced, who wait until the time is right or expect things to correct themselves or wait for someone to come to their aid.

Ways of cooperating in evil

Chastity and modesty are 'taboos' of old, backward civilisations full of heavy conventions which must now give way to the rights of eroticism; as regards priestly celibacy it is amazing how much pressure is put on the Church to force it to take a retro-gressive step which would deprive it of one of the most refined results of the spirit of the Gospel; the cinema can survive only if all censorship is suppressed, only if all guards go, even though th ese lead to corruption. Even intellectuals and university people become part of the crowd and opt for its anonymity. In the name of welfare and sexual rights children are murdered by abortion; the path to life is closed to those who ought to have been allowed to walk it — closed so that those who have lived and still live can enjoy the sacrosanct rights of sex without the risk of their standard of living falling and their having to share what they have with those who might have been.

A deafening noise blares through newspapers, magazines, lectures, meetings, books, pamphlets, advertisements: the whole complex machinery reinforces the noise of the means of com-munication in the name of the 'right to be informed.'

Crucify him! And Christ and his Church are crucified and those who say they believe in him shout along with the rest (most do it cunningly; others, sillier people or more full of themselves, do it so brazenly that you begin to wonder whether they are not really against Christ and his Church; they co-operate in evil, like little ants, with no clear ideas in their heads and no desire to acquire any, sometimes because they are too bored to, at other times because if they were to acquire them they know they would feel obliged to do all sorts of awkward things which they are not ready to do, even for the sake of their salvation. Those who are in positions of authority (and I am not really referring to governments, although it also applies to governments) do not know how or when or in what direction to exercise their authority, or perhaps they are too taken up with more important things and, like Pilate, just drift along in the direction which all the shouting points to. Could the Jewish authorities not argue that 'public opinion' had condemned Jesus?

That's how the crucifixion of Christ came about. Maybe many of those poor devils who had shouted in the praetorium and later when they saw what they had done beat their breasts, became disciples of Christ months afterwards, when Peter spoke to the crowd (in very clear terms, as we see in the *Acts of the Apostles*) and one day some three thousand five hundred were baptised. They were humble enough to realise their fault and upright enough to confess it.

But we continue being a mass which does not think; with the docility of a flock of sheep we cooperate actively in slow but sure ways, in spreading theories, ideas, fashions and life-styles which are destroying Christian values in society and eroding the teaching of the Gospel in people's consciences. Just as cowardice and stupidity made possible the great crime of the crucifixion, our cowardice and our stupidity open the way in our own time to the crucifixion of our Mother the Church. God grant that for our own good we one day come to realise the evil we have done and also beat our breasts in repentance.

Catholics and the Church

If you read in some book that the Son of God came to the world to found a Church, the almost instinctive reaction is to think that such a statement is wrong, that it goes too far. That God became man and lived among us, allowed himself to die hanging on a piece of wood and then rose from the dead only to found a Church, seems an odd wastefulness on God's part. What need was there for God to become man to do what any man could have done? Without having to go way back to Buddha and Confucius, or back to the less remote time of Mohammed, or to the more recent time of Luther and Calvin, we have John Wesley near us, founder of the Methodist Church, or more recently, Fox and the Quakers. And, in the last century, there was William Miller (corrected by Ellen White) who founded the Seventh Day Adventists and Joseph Smith, who in 1831 established the Mormon Church, or Mary Baker Eddy and her 'Christian Science,' and it was only yesterday (1931) that the Church of Jehovah's Witnesses was born by the hand of C.T. Russell. And this, just to mention the better-known churches.

Of course, if you consider the Church simply as an assembly of persons who believe more or less in the same things and are governed by the same rules, then there is no doubt that it is reasonable to think that there was no need for the Son of God to become man by assuming our nature, just in order to found his Church. Now, if this is what you think, don't broadcast it because you could confuse others and give them a poor (and mistaken) concept of the Church.

The Church of Jesus Christ is not only more than that, but above all something completely different. If you read the Old Testament (which cannot be separated from the New) you will see that it contains the history of the people of God. Having chosen Abraham as instrument and with the salvation of man as his goal, God made a people for himself out of the descendants of Abraham (although not all of them) and established a covenant with them, and then he revealed himself gradually to them. That is how it started — the preparation of mankind for the supernatural world, which it had lost through the sin of Adam. Slowly humanity was being educated through the chosen people, preparing it for the coming of the Son of God, who was to restore order and harmony in man and in the created world, both of which had been destroyed by sin. This was the Old Covenant established on nature and formalized by circumcision.

But the covenant and the people were transitory; they were merely a preparation, a figure, a shadow, a means toward a New Covenant that was to be both total and definitive. Jesus Christ established this new covenant with a new people of God. It is not founded, as the old one was, on nature, but on grace. It is not bound by flesh and blood but by the faith in Jesus Christ. One belongs to it not by an accidental and extrinsic rite but by the radical and intrinsic renewal which takes place in man through baptism, the death of the old man and the birth of a new man.

This new people of God partakes of the divine life, the same life by which Christ lives, and is also his mystical Body, a Body of which he is the head, and the baptized (that is, we), children of God by adoption, his members. How could a mere man ever do such a thing? A Church made up of the people of God, the mystical Body of Christ, with a life that is not natural (but supernatural); a Church which is the Sacrament of salvation: only God, as you can imagine, could found it, because no one but he could save men.

Well, I do not doubt that this is known by Catholics, although I don't know if by all. But a knowledge that is not made alive is a dead knowledge. It is a knowledge which is so sterile that it does not save but increases one's burden of responsibility.

I think that the Jews or, rather, some of them did not quite understand what the covenant and being the chosen people really meant, if we take the texts of the prophets into account. They turned the covenant into a sort of give and take contract and, instead of allowing themselves to be moulded by the Law of Moses, they used it as a shield to protect themselves from God's demands. I am afraid that a good many Catholics, perhaps the most conspicuous, have a similar attitude toward the

Gospel and toward the Church. It is more like the attitude one has toward an insurance company than toward a supernatural organism to which one is irrevocably committed, of which one has become a part and for whose lot one is responsible.

Hypocrisy

Indeed, there are Catholics for whom the main thing is not 'to have life' (that is, to be in the state of grace) but to fulfil their Church 'obligations.' As punctually as they pay their insurance premiums, they fulfil their religious duties (what they understand as 'religious duties'); they hear Mass on Sundays and holy days of obligation; they baptize their children; they are married in the Church; they go to confession (is it to reform or to be able to accompany a first-communicant child without actually changing one's own life?) . . . In exchange they are entitled to eternal life. This is the type of Catholic who is proud of being so (this is the true religion!) and is satisfied with his loyalty to the Church. On the other hand, he is indulgent toward human nature and, in the same way that he pays tribute to his religion, he pays tribute to natural weakness by committing sin (his weaknesses, he usually calls them). Not that he is proud of his sins. He simply understands them and he excuses himself. These Catholics give what they ought, what is expected of them (they think they do), although laying more stress on the commandments of the Church than on the Law of God: but not a lot more than what they consider necessary or obligatory. They do not want to be damned, that's for sure, because it would be very bad business; but neither are they interested in becoming holy because holiness demands many renunciations and they also regard renunciation as very bad business. More apparent than real, more external than internal, more formal than sincere, more interested in being saved than in loving God and their neighbours, they fulfil the Law to the letter but they are not interested in its spirit: they look more like the Pharisee than like the publican or the disciple. What Jesus said of his own people could be said of them: 'This people honours me with their lips, but their heart is far from me' (Mt 15:8).

I think that this is (if I've described it well) the type of Catholic whom young people do not like, supposing they like anybody. Today's young people detest that kind of propriety. They simply abhor and rebel against duplicity and hypocrisy, empty conventional formulas and the self-satisfied attitude of those who think themselves good. I feel, however, that if the college student thinks himself better for getting out of such a scene, it would be worth while for him to reflect a little and try to discover the root of his own self-satisfaction.

For, is that type of religiosity what he rejects? Or is that type of religiosity the cloak which covers, and in his own eyes, justifies his own desertion from all his duties to God?

'Hypocrisy is the tribute that vice pays to virtue,' someone said not long ago. But I don't see any reason for satisfaction in the fact that vice no longer pays any tribute to virtue or that, in the name of sincerity or authenticity, sin is exhibited as a triumph over the 'taboos imposed in the past', or as a liberation from absurd 'complexes' (modesty, decorum) or from 'old and conventional' moral rules.

Solidarity

If our knowledge were vital knowledge, a knowledge translated into life, our behavior would be really very different. If we are a Body ruled by the Head, by Christ, we are in solidarity with one another, whether we like it or not. This means that whatever any of us does or fails to do is never a merely personal matter, since it reverberates in the entire Body, in the entire Church, in all the others, just as a toothache is not something which affects only a part of one's mouth, but bothers the whole person. Thus, every sin causes a real damage to the Church and thereby to the rest of us, to the entire Body. Every disobedience — that is, every act against the will of Christ — is a separation, a step toward disunity, an injury therefore to the entire Body. In contrast, every good deed (and it is good to the extent that it is wanted and, therefore, shared by Christ) adds to the solidity and unity of the Church and health of the Body, and its good infleunce reaches up to the last corner. In short, this means that when a Catholic ignores the community of which he is part as member of a Body, in order to live his life independently, then he becomes a cancer that corrodes the organism and hastens its death.

Of course, the Church cannot be killed. But she can certainly be wounded each time one of her members is killed or wounded. She cannot be killed for she is indestructible. However, we can cause her many injuries; and, in fact, that is what we are doing. She, the Church, is holy; but we, her children, are not, and anyone who has eyes and can see with them will be able to perceive this; our behaviour often causes scandal and discredits the Church.

There is, of course, a very simple way to avoid this grave harm and remove the scandal produced by the behaviour of many Catholics who turn their backs on their faith, or ignore it, or oppose it while paying lip-service to it: those who have decided in fact to enjoy to the maximum the pleasure and comforts of this earth, or who accommodate the Gospel to their own likings, and leave it for the last moment to come to terms with God and thus secure their salvation in the last minute (so they hope) by means of a rushed confession. This simple way would be for the Church to expel from her bosom all those who are not holy and who do not show the slightest desire to be; all those who take advantage of her, without giving her anything; all those who, because they habitually live in the state of mortal sin, are dead. Then the Church would be holy, both in herself and in all her members, and her light would not be dimmed by the dirt caused by the sins of her children. As you can imagine the Church cannot do that, because she is the Sacrament of salvation and only for the salvation of the entire Body has the Church been forced sometimes to take this step as a bitter medicine. The Church is a Mother and instead of expelling those who do her harm and who hurt her, she holds them in order to give them life, for her hope is inexhuastible. She holds them close to herself in order to do them good, but they soil her, dishonour and humiliate her (Leclercq).

This is no exaggeration. In a letter to his bishop in 1841, Newman expressed what perhaps many others were thinking without daring to say it: 'Until Catholics . . . do not manifest in their public behaviour the light of holiness and truth, we will war against them.' We are one of the causes (and perhaps the main one) why the Church is not really known or understood, why she is despised or why she is accused of hypocrisy. I even wonder if we could not apply to us Catholics of today (to all of them, not only to the 'adults') that terrible accusation of St Paul of the Jews: 'For the name of God . . . is blasphemed through you among the Gentiles' (Rom 2:24).

It is certainly our fault. I suppose that the good atheists who see the spectacle of many of the Catholics of the 'free world' must think that it is not worth the effort even to inquire what truly is there in the Church: a good tree cannot produce such bad fruit. And it seems understandable to me that young people, seeing the sometimes fairly grotesque conventionalism of many Catholics, may feel the sting of doubt, and be tempted to look elsewhere for something that could quench that thirst for truth, for purity and for goodness, which all of us feel.

Criticising the Church

I don't know how much good there is in that anxiety to improve things which has led us to intone a groaning *mea culpa* with great publicity, with the added conviction that we have thus let a gust of 'fresh air' come into the Church which is going to purify and renew her. This public atonement expresses itself in two ways. One of them is to lambast, to denounce the Church's 'defects.' It seems that the old saying that 'dirty linen is washed at home' has lost its force and now the stains that soil the Church are shouted out to the winds or denounced to the world. What I cannot quite understand is what good can be done to anybody by the publication and morbid exhibition of those miseries, especially if we take into account that *it is we* that have smeared the face of the Church beyond recognition. It is not the Body — the Church as such — but its members, who, with a crafty way of taking advantage of our religion, are the very stains that we denounce to her face. The Church is holy, even if we her members are very far from being so; it is a Church without sin, but not without sinners. But we prefer publicity to put her to shame than to acknowledge our own shame and be willing to carry it.

On the other hand, there is a tendency to 'help' the Church by counselling her, in a supercilious and pontificating tone, on what she ought to do, what steps she should take at this time, so that we her children may not feel embarrassed by her being out of date with civilization. What is hard to understand, however, is by what authority and in whose name we publicly give lessons to those of whom Christ said 'he who hears you, hears me' (Lk 10:16). Perhaps he changed his mind and, instead of speaking to us through them, he speaks to them through us?

I don't think this is the way to observe the solidarity and interdependence to which members of the same Body are bound. To be a disciple of Christ, to be a son of the Church, means being always ready and willing to be moulded by the Gospel. It means being consistent with faith in Christ, whatever one may have to renounce for it. It means *committing* oneself irrevocably, consciously, deliberately, to a supernatural enterprise, dead or alive.

The Church is conservative and revolutionary

For one must realize that the Church is at once conservative and revolutionary. Indeed, the Church of Jesus Christ has necessarily to be conservative. She has to preserve the deposit of revelation whole and unchanged, since she exists for the precise purpose of guarding it and transmitting it in all fidelity. She has to preserve the full force of the sacraments, which are springs of supernatural life, and it is not in her power to suppress or add a single one, for they were instituted by Christ and the Church exists in order to administer them. She has to preserve the moral norms and teach them constantly to all mankind. She has to show the way of salvation and she cannot give in to any error in any of these norms, because that would be tantamount to compromising with sin and, therefore, to opposing redemption which would obviously run contrary to her own essence.

At the same time, the Church is 'revolutionary.' (I dislike using this word because it has been mishandled so often and because it is almost a cliché, usually employed superficially, but I think it is the most suitable one to make myself understood). 'Revolutionary': not in the banal sense of the word but in its genuine sense. The Church never says 'Enough' but demands always more. The Church, as the upholder of the doctrines of Jesus Christ, that is, of the Gospel, not only denounces an unjust and oppressive state which enslaves and corrupts man, but labours incessantly for the overthrow of that order brought about by sin, precisely, and for the installation of a just order where men will come to know one another as brothers, will come to know the truth and will live freely. By the very nature of things, the Church can never be satisfied. As you can see, she can never even look forward to seeing the moment when she can stop her fight and can rest with nothing more to do but to keep her acquisitions. This aspiration for an earthly messianic kingdom which the Pharisees had is today just about kept alive in Marxism. For Marxism only awaits the classless society (assuming, even if it is too much to assume, that such an expression is more than just one more utopia) in order to petrify itself into a conservatism without hope and without horizon.

But the Church believes neither in myths nor in fairy-tales. She knows that the injustice, tyranny and corruption in the world are the result of sin, and that sin is everywhere present among men in each of its forms — selfishness, lust, covetousness, anger, violence, deceit, injustice, hypocrisy, hate, falsehood, greed, laziness. The Church knows — Christ himself taught her — that sin was conquered on the cross and that men, through the cross of Christ and not by any other way, can purify themselves from its corruption. She knows also that a cleaner, a freer and a less false society is possible, but on condition that people strip themselves of their selfishness, whatever form it takes. That is why she demands of her faithful a series of virtues such as humility, charity, purity, honesty, renunciation, sacrifice, meekness, temperance, prudence, industriousness, fortitude, obedience, justice, compunction, good works, alms, etc. — virtues which are frowned upon by men such as Nietzsche as 'negative' virtues and also by many others for the mere fact of being virtues.

Now, the most painful wounds, the worst affronts which the Church has received up to now, have come from her own children. As long as we refuse to admit that personal sins (by action or by omission), those of each and everyone of us, are the cause of the stains, defects and ineffectiveness that we usually criticize in the Church, we have not even begun to love her. In this sense, the contrast between us and the Catholics of eastern Europe is shocking. There, to be a Catholic means at best to live as a social outcast, almost without any rights; at other times, the risk of imprisonment and even of death. And the Church, the Sacrament of salvation, because of the fortitude and loyalty of these people continues existing in these countries as the light of hope, where the hope of a terrestrial bliss they used to have is now vanishing. There persecution has succeeded only in intensifying the fidelity of the faithful to the Church and to faith in Christ. But the wealth and well-being of the Western countries are bringing about the corruption (in minds and in morals) of so very many Christians that there seems to be no better way to achieve a general apostasy, at least in practice.

Young people and the Church

Despite all this, it is not too late. And in the renewal of the Church, the youth of today have a decisive role as well as a grave responsibility, because it is they who will characterize society ten or fifteen years from now. On their side they have their awareness of what should not be done, of what one cannot be, and their yearning, somewhat obscure but evidently real, for what is precisely the core of the Gospel. Against them they have their very defective education and an image of Christ, of the Gospel and of the Church so poor, shallow and grotesque that any resemblance to reality is mere coincidence. But if they take it seriously, if they search, if they ask, if they go deeply into it, if they reflect in inner silence, if they look for the truth . . . who knows? The road is difficult, because it demands sacrifice and renunciations; it demands becoming a new man. But the results are incalculable. And because the Church is the mystical Body of Christ and all of us are her members, in solidarity with one another, perhaps a little pondering on these words of Mgr Escriva in *The Way* could open up horizons enough to bring abut the change that God asks of all of us: 'Many great things depend — don't forget it — on whether you and I live our lives as God wants' *(The Way,* 755). On the other hand, if we continue doing our own thing and do not behave as God wants, only he knows what disasters we can bring about in this already badly mangled world.

Hail Mary

If you read the Christian literature of the early centuries you may well be surprised to find so few references to the Virgin Mary. Well, don't be. During her life on earth she was truly unnoticed and she was not going to show herself in those first centuries when the new-born Church had to teach revealed truth to a world populated by female deities of all sorts. She was loved and venerated by Christians from the very beginning, right from apostolic times, but the fame of her greatness had to wait until the world was ready to understand.

The panorama changed little by little and from the fifth century on (the Council of Ephesus) the pace of change increased. Her passing unnoticed was no longer necessary or good or desirable. From that time on the study of theologians and the piety of the ordinary faithful deepened in knowledge of the Blessed Virgin, of her role in Redemption, of her place among the People of God and of her motherly compassion for sinners (for us, for all men and women who have crucified and continue to crucify Christ, with our sins). All generations have called her blessed and all have had recourse to her.

Now it is not she who hides

Now it is not she who hides. At a time of great spiritual poverty she appeared at Lourdes to draw men back from a mortal abyss. Not much attention was paid her, I am afraid. She came again; this time at Fatima, and showed still greater anxiety than at Lourdes, insisting once more on the danger we were courting, even on earth, if we did not abandon our sinful ways. She was not heeded. So-called Christian and western civilisation does not seem over-interested in preserving its Christian title. Rather, it prefers to be known or characterised as the 'technological' or 'consumer' society.

No, it is not Mary who hides herself now. It is present-day civilisation which rejects her, relegates her to the shadows, distanced from human life and thought. And it does so for a good reason. Indeed, even with the best will in the world it is impossible to see how a society which commercialises sex to the extent of presenting eroticism and pornography as good, which tolerates and even promotes corruption, can find room for the Virgin Mary when the very mention of her name is an affront to every kind of impurity, filth, exhibitionism and immodesty. It does not seem easy for a society whose greatest values are money, pleasure and success at any price, to tolerate one who declared herself God's handmaid, who lived poor, passed unnoticed and embraced the Cross. For a society which has banished the notion of sin, she, the Refuge of sinners, cannot be a source of hope, but only an uncomfortable reminder of something it wants to forget. What can the Virgin Mary mean for a society which mocks virginity and extols adolescent sexual relations?

Little children need their mother

Today mankind boasts of having reached maturity; some Catholics too believe it and boast of having reached a Christianity which is likewise mature. But in the Gospel we are told that the kingdom of heaven belongs to those who are like children. There we read that Jesus, full of joy, praised his Father for revealing great things to the humble and to those who were children and for hiding them from the wise and powerful. And he told us also that if we did not become like little children we would not enter the kingdom of heaven. Now, we are children, we are small, to the extent that we continue to need our mother. Perhaps this is the reason why the 'adult' Christians of our time have relegated Mary to the attic and laugh condescendingly at foolish things like the month of May being dedicated to Mary, or the scapular of Carmel, treating them like things proper to under-developed Catholics?

I think it is a bad sign that the saying of the Rosary has been deliberately disparaged and that this devotion has been banished from many parishes and almost all schools. I think it is diabolic that, under the guise of ecumenism, de-mythologizing or whatever, one hides or conceals the virginity of the Mother of our Saviour as if it were a scar to be ashamed of. This is happening, even in widely-read books, published against, or at least without reference to, the wishes of the Holy See.

If devotion to the Blessed Virgin is a 'sign and pledge of salvation' (and the Church teaches that it is) then I fear that our days cannot be counted as a time in which the hope of salvation shines bright. I cannot help having the impression that our Christianity, cut off from Mary, no matter how adult, up-to-date and *aggiornato* it proclaims itself to be, is parched and cold. We feel orphaned if our Mother is missing from our lives. She is Mother of the Church as well, and a church which relegated her to obscurity could no longer be a home. It might be, perhaps, a community, an association, an assembly, but not the house of our Father, where a Mother gives each child the treasures gained for all by the First-born among all brethren.

Well, perhaps you are thinking that all that I am saying is very negative. And you are right. There is nothing positive in all these trends which tend to edge out the Blessed Virgin from theology, liturgy and even our personal devotions. But even so, they are signs of the times, and signs which we need to know of because they are an error we must avoid; they are symptoms of a state of health which is a cause for concern. I should not want you to think them advances in theology or a clearing away of dead wood which has hindered the progress of the Church for many centuries; in other words, I do not want you to abandon devotion to Mary.

A real basis for devotion to Mary

The fact is that devotion to her who is full of grace and blessed among women has a real basis. I mean, it is not something superfluous, an unnecessary adornment which has been over-exposed and needs to be put back in its right place. Whatever may be the theological or devotional trends of a given period, Mary will never cease to be the Mother of God. That almighty God himself chose her to give us, through her, his Son is always something meaningful, and never accidental. That a whole branch of theology is dedicated to studying the mystery of Mary is indicative of the need to take very seriously indeed her relationship with the work of redemption. The fact that Vatican Council II saw fit to include in one of its key dogmatic documents a whole chapter on the new Eve, the Mother of the Church, should give us food for thought on the importance with which the Church views her.

I realise that for many of you — I wish it were for all — there is no need to insist on this; you have always known it. But when some people seem bent on eliminating her from the interior life of Christians and on concealing her as much as possible within the whole panorama of the Catholic faith, it seems to me worthwhile to spend a few minutes correcting errors which could spell ruin for many souls. I am not exaggerating, I assure you: it could cause the ruin of many souls.

I am not going to go into detailed reflection about Mary. I have already done so for you, and in sufficient depth [a reference to his book *Mary of Nazareth*]. But I want to impress on you how much we need her. I just cannot understand (unless it is the direct work of the devil) how anyone can be put off by devotion and love for our Lady. Certainly, God the Father is not, who chose her from among all women to be the Mother of his Son. Nor is God the Son, Jesus Christ, who gave her to us as a Mother from the Cross, as one who in his last will and testament gives everything he possesses. Nor God the Holy Spirit who through the mouth of Elizabeth called her blessed.

How is it possible to believe that love for Mary, and the warm expression of that love in acts of piety, can be something which cuts us off from Christ or that distorts our piety or is displeasing to God? How can one think that devotion to Mary could ever be a problem when the Church has approved, encouraged, blessed and recommended such devotion for centuries? No, it is not a mere whim, or a compromise with popular piety or with the inevitable sentimentalism of poor, unenlightened faithful. On the contrary, it has deep theological roots, sunk into the fertile soil of the revealed word of God.

The surest, easiest and shortest way

Possibly the just — or those who believe they are just — can do without her. But we, you and I, are sinners; and because we are sinners we can never imagine that she could take away from her divine Son; no, just the opposite, we *know* that she is, and has always been and will always be, the surest, easiest and shortest way of reaching him. Nobody is so grown-up as never to need to lean on another; nobody is so powerful — not even the Pharisees who allowed themselves the luxury of rejecting the salvation offered them — as to be self-sufficient; all of us, at some time in our life, need help. The thing is, though, that some accept the help and others do not.

We sinners know that she is the Refuge, who never tires of giving us her hand, time and again, as often as we fall and make an effort to get up. Those of us who go through life jumbling and faltering, who are so weak that we cannot avoid the pitfalls to which human nature is inclined: we know that she is the comforter of the afflicted, the refuge where, as a last resort, we can find peace, serenity, and the kind of consolation which only a mother can give and which can set things right again. We know also that in those moments when our helplessness reaches almost exasperation and despair, when nobody can do anything and we feel absolutely alone with our suffering or our shame, cornered in a blind alley, she is still our hope, she is light in the darkness. She is the one to have recourse to when there is nobody else.

I think that this is what Francis Jammes expresses so well in his poem, *Rosaire,* some of whose lines, rather freely translated, I cannot help but quote for you. I hope you will find in them what I have failed to express:

> For the little one
> who dies in the arms of his mother
> while the other children
> play in the garden;
> and for the wounded bird
> who knows not how,
> but feels his wing bleeding
> and falls.
> For the thirst and the hunger
> and for the burning cry,
> *Hail, Mary.*
>
> For those children beaten up
> by the drunkard who returns home;
> for the poor donkey
> whom they kick in the belly,
> and for the humiliation
> of the innocent who is punished;
> for the maiden who is sold
> and stripped,
> and for the children whose mother
> has been insulted,
> *Hail, Mary.*

For the old woman who stumbles
under a heavy load
and cries out, 'O God!';
for the unfortunate whose arms
cannot hold on
to a human love,
like the Cross of the Son
on Simon of Cyrene;
for the horse fallen
under the cart he is pulling,
Hail, Mary.

For the four horizons
that crucify the world;
for all those whose flesh
is torn or flags;
for those who are without feet,
for those who are without hands,
for the sick
who are operated on, and moan,
and for the just
placed on a par with murderers,
Hail, Mary.

For the mother who hears
that her child has been cured;
for the bird that remembers
the bird fallen from its nest;
for the grass that is thirsty
and receives the rain;
for the lost kiss,
for the regained love,
and for the beggar
who finds his coin,
Hail, Mary.